Myrtle Beach

Myrtle Beach

by
Fahmida Y. Rashid

TOURIST TOWN GUIDES™

Myrtle Beach (*Tourist Town Guides*™ series)
© 2007 by Fahmida Y. Rashid

Published by:
Channel Lake, Inc., P.O. Box 1771, New York, NY 10156-1771
http://www.channellake.com

Author: Fahmida Y. Rashid
Editor: Elisa Lee
Cover Design: Julianna Lee
Photos: Myrtle Beach Area Convention & Visitors Bureau, iStockphoto

Published in October, 2007

All rights reserved. Published in the United States of America. No part of this book may be reproduced or transmitted in any form or by any means, electronic or mechanical, including photocopying, recording, or by any information storage and retrieval system, without permission in writing from the publisher. *Tourist Town Guides*™ is a trademark of Channel Lake, Inc. All other trademarks and service marks are the properties of their respective owners.

ISBN-13: 978-0-9792043-6-4
Library of Congress Control Number: 2007929279

Disclaimer: The information in this book has been checked for accuracy. However, neither the publisher nor the author may be held liable for errors or omissions. *Use this book at your own risk.* To obtain the latest information, we recommend that you contact the vendors directly. If you do find an error, let us know at corrections@channellake.com.

Channel Lake, Inc. is not affiliated with the vendors mentioned in this book, and the vendors have not authorized, approved or endorsed the information contained herein. This book contains the opinions of the author, and your experience may vary.

For more information, visit http://www.touristtown.com

Help Our Environment!

Even when on vacation, your responsibility to protect the environment does not end. Here are some ways you can help our planet without spoiling your fun:

- ✓ Ask your hotel staff not to clean your towels and bed linens each day. This reduces water waste and detergent pollution.

- ✓ Turn off the lights, heater, and/or air conditioner when you leave your hotel room, and keep that thermostat low!

- ✓ Use public transportation when available. Tourist trolleys are very popular, and they are usually cheaper and easier than a car.

- ✓ Recycle everything you can, and properly dispose of rubbish in labeled receptacles.

Tourist towns consume a lot of energy. Have fun, but don't be wasteful. Please do your part to ensure that these attractions are around for future generations to visit and enjoy.

To John,
who gave me the time to work,
and to Zameen,
who waited patiently for me to finish.

COVER IMAGES

Front cover: a golf bag[1], the beach and the ocean[1], Murrell's Inlet[2];
Back cover: golfing in Myrtle Beach[2].

[1]Photo courtesy of **iStockphoto**
[2]Photo courtesy of **Myrtle Beach Area Convention & Visitors Bureau**

Channel Lake, Inc.
P.O. Box 1771
New York, NY 10156

Dear Readers,

Tourist towns are a fundamental part of many vacations. Year after year, visitors arrive in droves to enjoy unique attractions. Yet these same visitors are inundated with billboards and promotional flyers that can make even a well-planned trip confusing.

This is the purpose of the *Tourist Town Guides*™ series – to keep you informed with honest, independent advice about national and regional tourist hotspots. Use these guides to look beyond all that self-serving promotion.

Many travel books fail to give tourist towns the coverage they need. *Tourist Town Guides*™ helps make sure you have the necessary information, without unnecessary clutter. Thoughtfully researched and intuitively organized, the books in this series are your comprehensive guides to all things tourist.

I am confident that you will find these guides both informative and useful, and that you will refer to them again and again. Enjoy your vacation!

Sincerely,

Dirk Vanderwilt
Executive Editor
Channel Lake, Inc.

www.touristtown.com

*The **shag**, a kind of swing dance, got its start in the 1940s in Myrtle Beach and the Grand Strand.*

Table of Contents

Introduction	**17**
How to Use this Book	*18*
Myrtle Beach History	**23**
Area Orientation	**29**
Who Visits Myrtle Beach	*30*
Getting Information	*31*
Getting to Myrtle Beach	*33*
Getting Around Myrtle Beach	*35*
Planning your trip	*37*
Seasons and Temperatures	*40*
Online Resources	*44*
Annual Events	*45*
Beaches...	**53**
Water Recreation	*55*
Water Rentals and Activities	*57*
Boating	*60*
Fishing	*63*
Places to Fish	*67*
Golf	**71**
Golf Info and Organizations	*72*
Tournaments	*73*
Golf Courses	*76*
Par 3 Courses	*84*
Miniature Golf	*85*
Area Amusements	**89**
Museums	*90*

Amusement Parks, Water Parks	92
Nature	96

Parks and Recreation 99

State and City Parks	99
Fitness and Rentals	101
Spectator Sports	103

Entertainment 107

Shows	107
Fine and Performing Arts	113
Nightlife	114
Dancing	115
Sports Bars	117

Where to Eat 121

Seafood	122
Steakhouses	123
International	124
Elegant Dining	125
Casual Dining	128

Where to Shop 133

Outlets	134
Shopping Centers	135
Specialty Stores	136

Broadway at the Beach 139

Attractions	140
Fun Eating	143
Fun Stores	149
Nightlife	150

Accommodations 153

Inns with the Personal Touch	*155*
Resorts	*158*
Sands Resorts	*167*
Broadway at the Beach	*172*
RV and Campgrounds	*175*

Outside Myrtle Beach 183

North Strand	*183*
South Strand	*189*

Recommendations 197

Travel Scenarios	*197*
Author Recommendations	*203*

Index 209

Myrtle Beach
Ocean Boulevard - Kings Highway (US 17)

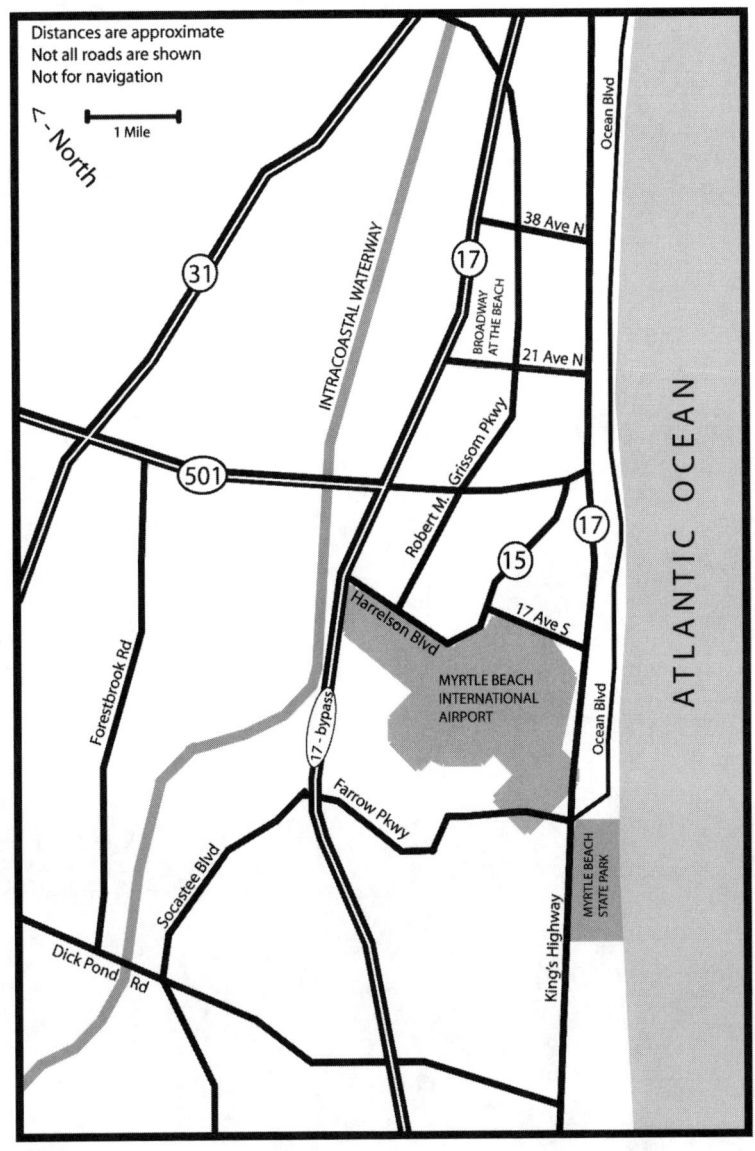

Introduction

Welcome to Myrtle Beach! With its beaches, golf courses, amusement parks, attractions, and theaters, Myrtle Beach is considered one of the nation's top vacation hotspots. Various tourism groups and magazines, including AAA, *Southern Living* magazine, *Wall Street Journal* and *Money* magazine, have named Myrtle Beach as a top family vacation destination and a popular choice amongst retirees.

The city of Myrtle Beach is located on the central area on the island of Grand Strand, off the coast of South Carolina. The Grand Strand is an island with 60 miles of oceanfront, extending from Calabash, North Carolina down south to Georgetown, South Carolina. Surrounded by the Atlantic Ocean on the east, Winyah Bay on the south, and the Intracoastal Waterway on the north and west, the island has three roads connecting it to the mainland. Untouched beach wilderness, salt marshes, classic Spanish moss, and hammocks co-exist alongside hi-tech amusement parks, golf courses, and entertainment theaters.

Visitors to Myrtle Beach can expect to enjoy a variety of activities, including swimming, sunbathing, sea shelling, volleyball playing, Sea-Dooing, fishing, parasailing, boating, and more. It's a place to relax and enjoy your holiday.

Located in Horry County, Myrtle Beach is the largest community in The Grand Strand. A major tourist destination on the South Atlantic seaboard and widely known for its wide beaches and a large selection of challenging golf courses, the city attracts over 14 million visitors a year. Although Pawley's Island, to the south, has been considered a vacation spot for the wealthy long before Myrtle Beach even existed, Myrtle Beach nowadays attract more visitors, especially amongst the general population.

A small city, the area of Myrtle Beach is only 16.8 square miles (43.5 square km). The city has the Atlantic Intracoastal Waterway on the west, and the Atlantic Ocean on the east. The area between the coast and the waterway is an elevated sandbar. West of the waterway is mostly pine forest with a normal high-water table. In recent years, construction has begun west of the Waterway, allowing the city to expand.

According to the US Census Bureau, the city's residents are predominantly white. Hispanic and Latinos are the second largest, even though they make up less than five percent of the population. Myrtle Beach's population also includes African Americans, Native Americans, Asians, and Pacific Islanders. While the city has a significant sect of senior citizens, they do not make up the largest group.

Located approximately halfway between New York City and Miami, the city itself is busy. Traffic is heavy, and crowds spill into the streets during the spring and winter. Tacky souvenir shops clamor for your business. But the city has something for everyone – a long swim in the Atlantic, the festive spirit of parties and shows, the peaceful serenity of the Intracoastal Waterway, and the challenge on the golf course – all year-round.

How to Use this Book

Items are listed within subject groups. Based on information availability, the attraction may have an address, website (🖰), and/or telephone number (☎). Some items have other items within them (for example, a restaurant within a casino). In this case, the contact information may be with the inline text, or there may be no contact information. If there is no contact information, please see the attraction or section heading.

Must-See Attractions: Headlining must-see attractions, or those that are otherwise iconic or defining, are designated with the 🔲

symbol. The author and/or editor made these and all other qualitative value judgments.

Coverage: This book is not all-inclusive. It is comprehensive, with many different options for entertainment, dining, eating, shopping, etc., but there are many establishments not listed here. Since this is an independent guide, the decision of what to include was made entirely by the author and/or editor.

Attraction Pricing: When applicable, at the end of each attraction listing is a general pricing reference, indicated by dollar signs, relative to other attractions in the region. The scale is from "$" (least expensive) to "$$$$" (most expensive). Contact the attraction directly for specific pricing information. **Please note that** if the attraction is free, of if no pricing information is available at the time of publication, or if a price indication is otherwise irrelevant, then the dollar sign scale is omitted from the listing.

"Family Friendly" Designations: This book mentions attractions that may have a "family friendly" attitude. *However*, this does *not* guarantee that the attraction meets any kind of standards for you or your family. It is merely an opinion that the attraction tends to be acceptable to some families as being appropriate for children. You are urged to contact all establishments directly to avoid possibly exposing your children to something inappropriate.

Based on the number of visitors annually, **Broadway at the Beach** *is South Carolina's most popular single tourist attraction.*

Myrtle Beach History

As the area's first inhabitants, the Waccamaw and Winyah Indians called the area, Chicora, which means, "the land." Many of their names live on in the rivers and bays. An Indian burial mound can be found on Waites Island, near Little River (see "Venturing Outside of Myrtle Beach" for details on this village).

While the Europeans attempted to settle this area, the section that is now Myrtle Beach remained uninhabited until the early 1900s. Most settlement happened along what is now referred to as South Strand. English colonists planned Georgetown, the Grand Strand's southernmost point, in 1730. It became the center of colonial America's rice empire. The "Venturing Outside of Myrtle Beach" chapter lists still-standing rice plantations to visit.

What is now the US Highway 17 and the section of it known as Kings Highway was originally an Indian trail. During the colonial period, the trail evolved into a stagecoach route from the northern colonies to Charleston (South Carolina) and Savannah (Georgia).

Pirates used the bays and inlets of the Grand Strand to hide their activities. Locals like to tell stories about Blackbeard harassing local shippers and about Captain Kidd's buried treasure. During the American Revolution, Francis Marion, the South's legendary guerrilla leader, spent time navigating the various rivers, bays, swamps, and marshes along what is now known as the Intracoastal Waterway. As the "Swamp Fox," Marion based his operations among the waterways and launched successful attacks on the British troops.

Pawley's Island, just north of Georgetown, is the Grand Strand's original vacation spot and one of the first resorts in the United States. The island, a half mile wide and four miles long, was dotted with summer cottages. The wealthy plantation owners and their families treated Pawley's Island as their summer retreat.

Until the 1900s, the area north of Murrells Inlet remained practically uninhabited. The area that became Myrtle Beach and the rest of North Strand was geographically inaccessible. While a salt-making facility operated in this area before it was destroyed during the Civil War, there was very little economy in this area.

F. A. BURROUGHS

Myrtle Beach can trace its creation directly to entrepreneur F.A. Burroughs, who bought some timberland several miles inland from the coast. The coastal area, at the time called Long Bay, was included in the deal. Burroughs and New York stockbroker S.G. Chapin teamed up to securing funding to develop the area into a resort to rival Pawley's Island. Mrs. Burroughs renamed Long Bay to Myrtle Beach because it sounded more attractive, after the rows of myrtle trees growing in the area.

In 1901, Burroughs' son, F.G. Burroughs constructed the area's first motel, Seaside Inn, in what eventually became the city's downtown area. Myrtle Beach did not have many visitors (let alone the rich and famous!) in those early years other than Burroughs' and Chapin's extended families.

RISE IN TOURISM

The city got a boost in 1908 when the railroad came to Myrtle Beach. At the time, the line connected Conway to Pine Island. The track was extended four miles to bring it into Myrtle Beach. Burroughs and Chapin formed the Myrtle Beach Farms, Inc. in 1912 to develop the area.

The original Pavilion amusement building was built in 1912. In 1925, a resort playground hotel with the city's first golf course was built for the rich and famous. The luxurious Ocean Forest Hotel featured chandeliers and an enormous ballroom.

The venture, however, fizzled with the stock market crash of 1929 and was finally demolished in 1974.

The first major route into the Myrtle Beach area, US Route 17, ran from the North Carolina border to the Myrtle Beach area and turned west and north into Conway. In 1934, US 17 was extended further into South Carolina. The road from Myrtle Beach to Conway was later renamed US 501. The new road system improved the region's accessibility.

The city grew slowly, but by the 1930s, it had expanded into the north part of Grand Strand. The Intracoastal Waterway began construction around this time. In 1938, Myrtle Beach was incorporated as a town in 1938. It became a city in 1957.

The Burroughs and Chapin Company (currently the owners of Broadway at the Beach) continued to operate small hotels and cottages, rent and sell land, and develop beachfront attractions. Burroughs sold parcels of land in the area for $25 a piece to build resort cottages.

Perhaps the most famous Myrtle Beach attraction was the Pavilion Amusement Park. Built on the original site of the 1912 amusement building, it was located in the heart of downtown, along Ocean Boulevard. The amusement park opened in 1948 and the rides had names like Siberian Sleigh Ride, Mad Mouse, and Hydro Surge.

In 1954, Hurricane Hazel destroyed the city. In order to survive, the city shifted its focus from attracting the rich and famous to become a vacation destination for the working class. The city built a new boardwalk and a modern pavilion to replace the bathhouses constructed in 1909 and The Pavilion built in 1912. Small mom-and-pop hotels, amusement parks, and minor regional attractions also appeared in Myrtle Beach. Soon the city became the tourist destination of choice for the hundred thousands of blue-collar families from the Carolinas.

US 501 was updated in the 1960's to accommodate the growing traffic coming into Myrtle Beach. Around this time, the North Strand began to be more developed as more communities (North Myrtle Beach, Briarcliffe Acres) were formed.

A building boom hit the area in the 1970s as hotels and beachfront attractions sprang up overnight. US 17 Bypass was built in the 1970s to handle the increased traffic and allow visitors to avoid Kings Highway when going from the city's northern limits to US 501. The building boom also created a new Myrtle Beach suburb: Surfside Beach. The same boom helped the city's suburb to the north, North Myrtle Beach, to grow. The Myrtle Beach International Airport terminal was built in 1975 and opened the following year with joint civilian-military use.

During the 1980s, Myrtle Beach expanded at a rapid rate and had the 18th largest population gain in the United States. The city was seeing increasing numbers of non-native residents amongst its population. Many of them were from the Northeast, who discovered the city's relatively low cost of living and mild climate during their vacations. While tourism continued to swell the city's population, these snowbirds became a significant portion of the city during this decade.

Hurricane Hugo hit in 1989, but again the Grand Strand rebounded. Building continued apace as new hotels and attractions were built. The city slowly moved away from the neon and glitz of the 1980s to a more natural look and feel.

Broadway at the Beach opened its doors in 1995. The entertainment mega complex combined both glitzy and charming features for an all-day experience. The success of the complex helped attract more tourists and smaller (but just as worthwhile) establishments into the area.

While the number of golf courses has now reached more than 120, the building boom has had some negative effects on the sport. In recent years, the soaring real estate prices have made it harder for golf courses to remain open. With Myrtle Beach developing rapidly and new buildings being constructed everyday, many of the independent golf courses have either closed down completely, or closed down portions of the course to make room for condominiums.

The Pavilion Amusement Park drew crowds for 58 glorious years until it finally closed on September 30, 2006. Attendance at the 11-acre amusement park had been declining for the past few years, and the park showed it in streak of rust or chipped paint on some rides. Burroughs & Chapin Company (still around!) plan to build a new shopping/dining/entertainment complex on the site.

Currently, Myrtle Beach attracts roughly 14 million visitors annually. Dozens of ambitious projects are in progress. Hard Rock Park, a $400 million theme park will be opening April 2008 at the old Fantasy Harbor-site along US 501 and Intracoastal Waterway. The amusement park, tied in with the Hard Rock Café restaurant, will have over 40 rides and attractions.

The city continues to reinvent itself to attract more people to play.

Area Orientation

As Atlantic coast vacation destinations go, there are a lot to choose from. And many of them are pretty much the same. There are public and private beaches, countless bars and restaurants, amusement parks, tourist attractions, hot sidewalks, out-of-place tropical trees, and tremendous traffic. Sure, they all have their unique aspects – gambling, amusement parks, golf. What sets Myrtle Beach apart is less about its uniqueness. What makes the area unique is that there is a lot of it. *A lot.*

Myrtle Beach, and indeed the entire Grand Strand, is a sprawling landscape of urban beach paradise, and everything that goes with it. If there is something about Atlantic coast beaches that you like, chances are you'll find it – a lot of it – in Myrtle Beach.

THE GRAND STRAND

On the eastern coast of the South Carolina is a stretch of sandy beach that has become – in many ways – the American answer to a tropical paradise. The 60+ miles of beaches, dotted with towns and developments both large and small, have become a haven for the vacation enthusiast. In addition to the beach, which sprawls seemingly endlessly and is the most popular draw, visitors come for golf, for spring break, and everything in between. It is hot in the summer and mild in the winter, and popular year-round. And in the middle of it all sits the epicenter of South Carolina tourism – Myrtle Beach.

WHO VISITS MYRTLE BEACH

Although there really is something for everyone in Myrtle Beach, this section describes a few of more popular "clicks" of tourists that make the trek.

GOLF ENTHUSIASTS
Surprisingly (or maybe not so much), the primary Myrtle Beach image is that of a sand trap, not a sandy beach. The area's many, many professional and world-class golf courses draw almost year-round attention to themselves as an almost steady stream of golfers make their way onto the courses. In fact, the Grand Strand, including Myrtle Beach, has the highest concentration of public golf courses in the world, with well over 100. Tournaments abound.

WATER SPORT ENTHUSIASTS
The beach is right in front of your nose. Millions of people come just to enjoy the many watery wonders that the Grand Strand has to offer. And there are *lots* of these wonders. The beaches are mostly clean, the water can be very warm (over 80° F in the summer), and a slew of rental equipment shops allow even the fair-weather fans to rent the equipment they need for a day of boating or more.

THE "SPRING BREAK" CROWD
While not the epitome of Spring Break locations, the clustered, quasi-urban environment offers enough summertime bliss for the older teen or college-aged kid to get very involved in what seems to be a perpetual summertime party. Law enforcement and neighborhood watch groups are able to control some of the inappropriate activities, but when such an influx of (primarily local)

party-goers find their way to the beach and area clubs, be prepared to deal with some pretty rowdy crowds.

FAMILIES
Somewhere in the mix of families of golfers and children who only like mini-golf, Myrtle Beach has blossomed a bit into a kind of family vacation destination in recent years. While many attractions are far from wholesome, there is enough here to occupy a wide range of younger tastes. The beach and resort swimming pools are popular; water and amusement parks are everywhere, and some pretty eclectic attractions have made themselves family-friendly. Older children (over about age 10) will have more fun at Myrtle Beach than the real youngsters.

GETTING INFORMATION

The more you know about Myrtle Beach before you go, the more you can do, and the more fun you'll have. Not only will you better appreciate your time, the anticipation of seeing the sights will be that much greater.

MYRTLE BEACH AREA CONVENTION AND VISITORS BUREAU
(1200 N Oak St ☎ 800.496.8250 ⌐ myrtlebeachinfo.com) The Myrtle Beach Area Convention and Visitors Bureau is a division of the Myrtle Beach Area Chamber of Commerce. The visitor's center provides maps, bus schedules, and information on shows, golf courses, and accommodations. There are also coupons and discounts available.

Much of the information provided by the Bureau is strictly promotional – that is, companies paid them to provide information about attractions and services. This information is of course biased, but it gives a good idea of the area's offerings.

INDEPENDENTLY PRINTED TRAVEL GUIDES

With few exceptions, printed travel guides tend to offer a lot more information than the vacationer needs, which may result in overcomplicated vacation planning. Certain high profile destinations such as Las Vegas and Orlando have many books devoted to that specific location. Myrtle Beach has several travel guides dedicated to both the city and the Grand Strand.

TRAVEL AGENTS

Commercial travel agents make planning vacations a breeze. They can search for the best deals, book flights and hotels, make restaurant reservations, and even make special requests on your behalf. Their most important asset, however, is their personal knowledge of the destination. They can recommend places to stay and things to see and do like no book or website ever could.

However, their service comes with its own price tag, which can be avoided by simply doing your own research – travel agents have no real greater power than a well-informed customer; they just have access to the right information.

THE INTERNET

Travel information constantly changes, and the Internet is a great way to keep up. Unfortunately, because of the largely level playing field of web sites, it is hard to know which sites to trust and which sites to examine with a bit more skepticism.

A definitive Internet source cannot be offered here; the best advice in learning about your destination of choice would be to (1) check multiple internet sources, including promotional sites, online travel agencies, and sites with user comments, and (2) check the "official" site, if any – official, meaning the site owned by the attraction or city you are interested in.

Getting to Myrtle Beach

Myrtle Beach's 14+ million visitors arrive using many common – and some less common – forms of transportation. Following is a breakdown of the best and most popular ways to arrive at the seaside destination.

BY PLANE

The **Myrtle Beach International Airport** (☎ 843.448.1589) is located on the former Myrtle Beach Air Force Base on the south side of town. The airport, located within city limits and less than five miles from downtown, opened in 1976. Even though the base has since then closed, the airport offers scheduled service by US Airways, as well as other major airlines, to and from over 200 domestic and international cities. While there are some direct flights, most flights come through Charlotte, North Carolina, or Atlanta, Georgia. Private or charter aircraft are available by calling **Myrtle Beach Aviation** at the airport (☎ 843.477.1860).

BY CAR

Driving remains the most popular way to visit Myrtle Beach. While traffic can get snarled and cars clog the main roads, having a vehicle remains the easiest way to get in and out of the city. Please keep in mind, however, that the city's main road, US 17, is a pretty slow road unless it's before 7AM or after 7PM. US 501 and beach exit roads are also pretty crowded between 7AM and 7PM.

For visitors coming in from eastern North Carolina, take Interstate 40 East, or US Highway 17 South to Wilmington, North Carolina. From Wilmington, continue southbound along US 17 into Myrtle Beach.

For visitors coming from Charleston, South Carolina, take US 17 North.

Northbound travelers on Interstate 95 can take exit 170, clearly labeled Myrtle Beach, and get on US Highway 76. The exit is near the city of Florence. From US 76, take US 501 into the city. Travelers on Interstate 20 should follow signs toward Florence, since the road will merge in I-95 North just before exit 170.

Southbound travelers on I-95 should take exit 193 at Dillon and head towards Latta to take US 501.

Visitors from western North Carolina, West Virginia, Ohio, western Pennsylvania, Michigan, and parts of Canada tend to use Interstate 77 and a network of state roads. This is a bit of a circular route, but it avoids narrow roads and traffic jams. The I-77 passes through Charlotte, North Carolina and goes to Rock Hill, South Carolina. From Rock Hill, take exit 77 onto US Highway 21 South and then head east onto SC Highway 5. SC 5 connects with US Highway 521. Head south to Lancaster, and then connect to SC 9, and then to SC 903. After about 20 miles, SC 903 connects to SC 151. SC 151 meets US 52 outside Darlington. US 52 goes towards Florence until it junctions with I-95.

BY BUS OR TRAIN

Greyhound [511 7th Avenue N ☎ 800.231.2222 ⌁ greyhound.com) buses stop near the downtown area. The bus line has specials from New York City (16-hour ride) and Atlanta (2-½-hour ride). More buses run to Myrtle Beach in the summer. The station is located on Oak Street and 7th Avenue North and is open from 10AM to 2PM and from 3:30PM to 7PM.

Amtrak (⌁ amtrak.com) does not come all the way to Myrtle Beach. The closest towns the train comes into are Florence and Dillon – but to finish the journey someone will either have to give you a lift or you will need to drive in. In the past, a

Greyhound service connected Florence and Myrtle Beach; the line was discontinued because of low demand.

BY BOAT

Boaters are welcome to use the **Intracoastal Waterway**. The Intracoastal Waterway follows a relatively parallel path with the Atlantic Ocean all the way from Boston, Massachusetts, to Key West, Florida. A 20-mile canal connects the Little River to the Waccamaw River, and goes right through the Grand Strand. Boaters can navigate their boats down the waterway and tie up at the marinas. The boating section of this book has information on local marinas.

GETTING AROUND MYRTLE BEACH

Getting around may be a little tricky until you realize that some streets have multiple names. Once you learn that, you will find it easier to orient yourself and find your destination.

The major roads run north and south, parallel to the Atlantic Ocean. The easternmost street is Ocean Boulevard. The next main road is Kings Highway, which is also commonly referred to as US 17 or Business 17. The next road to the west is US 17 Bypass, also called Alternate 17. The Bypass starts from Murrells Inlet and extends northward until it merges with Kings Highway just south of Restaurant Row.

Ocean Boulevard intersects with numbered avenues going east west, from 30th Avenue South to 1st Avenue South, and from 1st Avenue North to 82nd Avenue North. Various kinds of accommodations cluster along the south end of the boulevard. The central section of the boulevard features tourist-driven activities. An exclusive residential neighborhood starts from about 32nd Avenue North. Hotels and condominiums dominated the beachfront from 52nd Avenue North and further north.

Kings Highway and US 17 are connected by 21 Avenue N. The five-lane Oak Street makes going to the Myrtle Beach Convention Center easier from 21 Avenue North and 29 Avenue North. The Robert M Grissom Parkway is a four-lane route going from 48th Avenue N to Harrelson Boulevard near the airport. Many of the businesses, shopping centers, and shops line Kings Highway. Oak Street is primarily a business district.

BY CAR OR TAXI

The easiest and most accessible way to get around town is to drive. However, parking can be difficult or expensive (or both, especially downtown). Taxis are available – you can have your hotel or restaurant call for you to arrange a pickup, or you can call them yourself – but the fares aren't cheap. While taking a taxi spares you the trouble of looking for parking, the fares can easily add up. Many well-known rental car agencies have branches around Myrtle Beach and at the airport.

ON FOOT

Myrtle Beach is not very friendly to walkers. While the main drag, Ocean Boulevard, is easy to walk on, getting anywhere not on the boulevard is difficult. Many of the major roads, like Robert Grissom Way, do not have sidewalks and walking inland from Ocean Boulevard to Costa Grande Mall or Broadway at the Beach is a long walk. Many of the streets and hotels are also not very accessible by strollers or wheelchairs. Unless you plan your trip to be centered on a tiny area – such as Ocean Boulevard – you'd better prepare a non-walking way to get around.

BY PUBLIC TRANSPORTATION

The city has a **Coastal Rapid Public Transport** (☎ 843.488.0865 ✆ coastrta.com) bus service system that goes around the city. Fares are a dollar per passenger, and children under age five ride free. There are no transfers between buses; each bus takes a dollar per passenger. The buses run infrequently, usually once every hour. System schedules for the buses are available at all Myrtle Beach Convention Center [21st Street] offices. The Visitor's Centers scattered around town do not have them, but the main Visitor's Center at Broadway at the Beach [21st Avenue and 29th Avenue], located behind the Build-a-Bear Workshop does.

The bus tends to stop in front of hotels or major destinations, such as Broadway at the Beach and the Children's Museum.

PLANNING YOUR TRIP

When planning your trip to Myrtle Beach, you may feel overwhelmed with the sheer number of lodgings and accommodations available. Along with the hotels, resorts, motels, bed-and-breakfasts, and inns, the city also has condominiums and houses available for rent. The hotels and such often offer discounted rates for long stays, for a week, a month, the whole winter. The condominiums generally require a one-week rental.

Despite all the options, don't leave home without reservations – especially in the summer. Most places are packed full with no vacancies during the summer, the city's high season. Off-season for accommodations refers to the fall and winter.

Most hotels in the downtown area will not allow pets in the rooms; city law prohibits animals in public, especially downtown, from March to September. If you are planning on traveling with your animal companion, select a hotel outside the downtown area, and make sure to ask the hotel if it is pet-friendly. Some hotels also have relationships with local kennels.

When planning your trip, keep in mind that packages may help drop the cost of your entire vacation. Interested in catching a show while in town, or hitting a ball or two down the fairway? Consider getting a package – most packages combine accommodations, activity, and at least one meal (usually breakfast).

While there is no shortage of places to eat in Myrtle Beach, keep in mind that the city is not primarily a seafood town. Yes, most restaurants serve seafood, but if you are looking for specialties, consider going to other parts of Grand Strand. Most places serve at least one or two vegetarian courses, but the menu tends to be primarily meat-oriented. Ethnic cuisine, such as Thai, Japanese, and Mediterranean, are harder to find, but available. You don't have to worry about dressing for dinner, unless you are planning to go to one of the more up-scale places. The restaurant listings in this book try to indicate whether or not dressy attire is required.

While Myrtle Beach is the most crowded during the summer, there are also other times during the year when crowds swell. A popular spring break destination for college kids, the city becomes a college town in the spring. For golf, the high season is actually the spring, not the summer, though one of the largest amateur golf tournaments in the country is held in August.

The cheapest time to visit Myrtle Beach is in the winter. However, many businesses close for the winter after Labor Day and do not reopen until some time after Easter. Although the city is gradually becoming a more year-round community, it's best to confirm that all the places (shows, attractions, lodgings) you are interested in going to, are open for the winter.

PET POLICIES

Visitors to Myrtle Beach with pets will find the city unfriendly to their animal companions. Most hotels in the downtown area will not allow pets in the rooms; city law prohibits animals in public from March to September. If your pet must accompany you on the trip, try to get a hotel outside the downtown area. The city ordinance was passed after visitors with exotic pets, such as iguanas and boa constrictors, showed them off in public. The law was passed to protect people from accidents involving these animals.

LOCAL PUBLICATIONS
The local daily newspaper is called **Sun News** (✆ myrtlebeachonline.com). The paper provides local and international news, stock market reports, weather forecasts, a classified advertising section, and a "kicks!" section that lists upcoming events and entertainment and reviews. Myrtle Beach also has the Myrtle Beach Herald (✆ myrtlebeachherald.com), a broadsheet newspaper that comes out every Thursday morning, and **Alternatives NewsMagazine** (✆ myrtlebeachalternatives.com), a magazine listing upcoming cultural events.

TAXES
Note: This is not tax advice. Myrtle Beach has several taxes and fees: a five-percent South Carolina state tax, a 16-cents per gallon gasoline tax, and a two-and-half-percent hospitality charge added on prepared food, admission (to shows and attractions), and accommodations (of less than 90 days).

MEDICAL INFORMATION
Note: This is not medical advice. If you are feeling ill or need medical attention, the following facilities will be able to help. The **Physician Referral Source** (✆ grandstrandmed.com/PhysRef.asp ☎ 843.692.1052) refers the caller to a local physician after listening to symptoms. There are also walk-in clinics if you need medical attention that is not serious enough to go to the hospital emergency room. Most clinics don't take insurance, Medicaid, or Medicare, but will accept traveler's checks, personal checks (from South Carolina residents only), and credit cards. The clinics routinely treat sunburn, heat rash,

heat exhaustion, cuts, sprains, broken bones, jellyfish stings, and sore throats. Some facilities have more complex services.

Access Medical Care (4810 North Kings Hwy; ☎ 843.497.7131) is a medical complex with all types of physicians and a limited pharmacy. Care Express at **Grand Strand Regional Medical Center** (809 82nd Pkwy ☎ 843.692.1770 ⌘ grandstrandmed.com; open seven days a week, 24 hours a day) is an urgent care clinic within the emergency department. **Doctor's Care Myrtle Beach** (1220 21st Avenue N; ☎ 843.236.6000; ⌘ doctorscare.com) open seven days a week, for extended hours) provides primary and urgent care, has an on-site lab and x-ray facility, and dispenses common medications.

Seasons and Temperatures

Myrtle Beach boasts a mild subtropical climate that makes it pleasant year-round. Temperatures soar and the humidity is at its highest during the summer, in July and August. Even then, the beach always has a soft and welcoming breeze.

The weather in the spring is comfortable, as long as you are not swimming. Spring is the best time for most outdoor activities, such as golf. In the summer, most days start off with a warm sunny morning that becomes a hot afternoon. A breeze helps cool off in the evening. Like the spring, autumn in Myrtle Beach is fairly mild, requiring only a light jacket or a sweater. Winter is not too cold, so a golf game is not out of the question. A light jacket is a must for most winter days, although there are occasional just-shirt days. Eve-

Myrtle Beach Water Temp (in F)

January	50	July	81
February	52	August	83
March	57	September	80
April	62	October	73
May	69	November	65
June	77	December	55

Src: South Carolina State Climatology Office

Myrtle Beach Avg. Rainfall (Inches)			
January	3.66	July	5.19
February	3.5	August	5.58
March	3.79	September	5.58
April	2.12	October	3.23
May	2.99	November	2.97
June	3.66	December	3.45

Source: South Carolina State Climatology Office

nings are chilly.

The city has an average of 215 days of blue skies and bright sunshine each year. Myrtle Beach expects about 46 days when the temperature exceeds 90° F (32° Celsius). Worried about not getting sun during the winter? Have no fear. On average, Myrtle Beach sees sunny days for half the month, or 15 days, in the winter. The average creeps up to 18 days during a summer month.

Annually, the city averages 72 rainy days. The wettest months are July and August, but there are (on average) 72 days a year with over one-tenth-of-an-inch of rainfall. The driest months are October and November.

The average annual temperature is a comfortable 64° (Fahrenheit; 18° Celsius). July's average temperature is 88° F (31° C) and January's is 56° F (13° C). The average humidity daytime is about 57 percent. There are 42 frost days, or when nighttime low temperatures drop below freezing, annually.

What's a trip to the beach without taking a dip? The water is relatively warm year-round, but swimming in the ocean in the winter is going to be on the cold side.

Myrtle Beach Avg Temp (F), High (Low)			
January	56 (37)	July	91 (72)
February	60 (39)	August	89 (71)
March	68 (46)	September	85 (64)
April	76 (53)	October	77 (54)
May	83 (61)	November	69 (46)
June	88 (68)	December	60 (38)

Source: South Carolina State Climatology Office

HURRICANES

Hurricane season at the Grand Strand begins June 1 and goes through November 30. While hurricanes are more likely during this period than at any other time of the year, sometimes years go by without any developing hurricanes. In fact, there've been only 37 hurricanes coming within 60 miles of Myrtle Beach in a 135-year-span.

Statistically, Myrtle Beach is brushed or hit by a hurricane every 3.65 years. However, the city has had an average resting span of 11.25 years between direct hurricane hits. Most hurricanes that hit the area develop over the Atlantic Ocean (as opposed to over the Gulf of Mexico).

The city has flood and hurricane preparation plans published on its website (cityofmyrtlebeach.com/hurricane.html). Information about evacuation routes and storm information can be obtained by calling **the Disaster Operations Center** (843.918.1400). Please note that this number is active only when a storm threatens.

Local radio and television stations will also publicize this information as soon as a hurricane watch is declared.

Please note that if you happen to be visitor during a hurricane, and an evacuation is announced, do not wait. In areas near the ocean (like Ocean Boulevard) the waters rise quickly and the roads may become impassable. If you are staying in a mobile home, be aware that even a tied down one could tip over in the strong winds.

WHAT TO PACK

Just before venturing out for a day on the sand, remember that the sun is strong enough at Myrtle Beach that you can turn pink in under an hour – sometimes even in 30 minutes. Even on cloudy or cool days, the sun's harmful rays make it through and can cause bad burns. Even the shade is not always enough protection, since the sun's rays reflect off the sand and water. Too much sun can send sunbathers to the hospital complaining of blisters, nausea, and excruciating pain.

Bring sun block lotion with a high sun protection factor –at least SPF 30 – and remember to apply it an hour before swimming, walking or bicycling (in other words, before you venture outside). Don't forget to reapply it regularly, especially if you are swimming or perspiring, even if it claims to be waterproof or sweat proof. It might not be a bad idea to avoid the sun altogether from noon to 4pm, which is the hottest part of the day.

Bring a bottle of aloe, in case you still end up getting burnt. The aloe will cool and soothe the skin. Always wear an effective waterproof sunscreen when playing in local waters. Reapply the lotion or gel often, all over your body, even if you are wearing a shirt and shorts. When clothing gets wet, fibers relax and allow the sun a direct hit on your skin.

Bring a hat with at least a 3-inch wide brim shields the head and hair. A visor is also effective in protecting your face. Good sunglasses will also protect your eyes. Take care of young children and babies by making them wear hats and applying sunscreen every few minutes. Put T-shirts on them if they will be in the ocean for a few hours.

Unbleached cotton, satiny polyesters, and silk absorb or reflect UV rays, making those clothes comfortable and most appropriate for a day in the sun. Crepe, viscoce, and bleached cottons allow the rays to pass through, directly hitting your skin. Dark tones are actually better at absorbing rays than whites and pastels. Also, look for tight weaves like cotton twill in the clothing you bring.

A bathing suit is a must if you plan on going to the beach, waterparks, or swimming in the hotel pool. You will also want flip-flops, sandals, or other comfortable shoes for walking around on the beach and in the mall. The last thing a vacation needs is sore feet. If you are planning on going dancing, even if it's checking out South Carolina's state dance, the shag, you might want to pack dancing shoes.

A water bottle should be handy, and drink often. With the heat, it is very easy to become dehydrated. Evenings can become chilly in the spring and fall, and it can get a little cold in the winter. So pack a light jacket for those months. A heavy winter coat is not necessary, even in January. But do consider packing some warm clothes, such as long-sleeved shirts and sweaters. Mild temperatures can occasionally take a nosedive into the cold, and the last thing you want to do is be stuck in shorts and t-shirts.

ONLINE RESOURCES

If going back and forth between different web sites does not appeal to you, use one of the many web sites devoted to planning the entire trip for you. These one-stop sites offer to take care of your plane tickets, car rentals, and hotel reservations. Web sites specific to booking trips to Myrtle Beach often arrange golf or entertainment packages as well.

MYRTLE BEACH AREA CONVENTION AND VISITORS BUREAU

(*myrtlebeachinfo.com)* The Myrtle Beach Area Convention and Visitors Bureau is a division of the Myrtle Beach Area Chamber of Commerce. The official visitors' site lists hotels and golf courses, but you have to contact them individually to make reservations. It's a site primarily geared towards planning, and offers many helpful tips and suggestions.

MYRTLE BEACH AIRPORT.COM

(*myrtlebeachairport.com)* This site searches through discount plane fares and offers discounts on lodgings, and car rentals. The lodging specials are usually a steal, so it's worth taking the time to look. Most of the hotels on this site are located along Ocean Boulevard. Golf packages are also available.

GOLF TRIPS

(☎ 800.819.2282 ⁂ myrtlebeachtrips.com) Specializing in planning golf vacations, with lodging, entertainment, and golf courses in one package, this site also offers discounted tickets for miniature golf. Other sites include **Myrtle Beach Golf** *(⁂ myrtlebeachgolf.com)* and **Travel Golf** *(⁂ travelgolf.com)*. These sites offer multi-day golf packages, with lodgings included. The accommodations are generally at hotels affiliated with the golf course.

ANNUAL EVENTS

The following Calendar of Events summarizes some of the things happening in the city throughout the year. Every month, there is some festival, concert, or sporting event happening in Myrtle Beach. The list is by no means comprehensive, but it can be a start when planning your vacation. The Chamber of Commerce, Myrtle Beach Convention Center, and the City of Myrtle Beach web sites all offer search features for specific types of events.

Occurring throughout the year is **Art in the Park** (Chapin Park; 16 Avenue N and Hwy 17 ☎ 843.448.7690), a fine arts and crafts festival sponsored by the Waccamaw Arts & Crafts Guild. Over 100 artists present a variety of works, from traditional oil paintings to abstract meal sculpture and art glass. Children's activities, along with ample food and beverage, round out the offerings.

LIFESTYLES EXPO (JAN)

(Myrtle Beach Convention Center, 2101 Avenue N ☎ 843.881.3676) The largest show of its kind along the South Carolina coast, the Myrtle Beach Lifestyles Expo provides information on real estate, health and community services, and investment options to senior citizens. As a retirement expo, the two-day event annually at-

tracts around 10,000 people as over 140 exhibitors offer cooking demonstrations, health, fitness, fashion and beauty seminars, prizes, and live entertainment. The exposition provides seniors with the information they need to adjust to living on Myrtle Beach. The expo is sponsored by Golden Times, a South Carolina magazine.

THE BUDWEISER GRAND STRAND BOAT SHOW AND SALE (JAN)
(Myrtle Beach Convention Center, 2101 North Oak St ☎ 843.357.3098 ⏠ grandstrandboatshow.com) The Grand Strand Boat Association presents the Grand Strand Boat Show. The three-day show takes place at the Myrtle Beach Convention Center, with an in-water display at The Marina at Grande Dunes.

The show features three days full of new boat displays, boating and fishing-related exhibitors, and seminars conducted by local fishing experts. There is also a separate fair for children, with activities such as a jumping booth, balloons, story time, and a petting zoo. There is an admission fee for adults and children. Children under six years of age enter free.

NAT'L SHAG DANCE CHAMPIONSHIPS (JAN-MAR)
(☎ 843.497.7369 ⏠ shagnationals.com) The preliminaries for this premier shag dance competition begin in January, and the finals are held in March. The first National Shag Dance Championships was held in March 1984. The longest running shag contest in the United States, winners have gone on to perform at special events, including the Charlotte Hornets (basketball) games, the Beach Ball Classic, the PGA Annual Banquet, and the Beach Music Awards. Sponsored by Colonial Mall, the contest is held at Studebakers located at 2000 North Kings Highway, Myrtle Beach, SC.

Awards are presented in Master, Professional, and Junior categories. The first championship was held in 1984, making this the longest running shag contest in the country. Past winners have gone on to perform at special events, including the Charlotte Hornets (basketball) games, the Beach Ball Classic, the PGA Annual Banquet, and the Beach Music Awards. Sponsored by Colonial Mall, the contest is held at a variety of locations around the city. Call or check the web site for the most current list of sites.

BI-LO MYRTLE BEACH MARATHON (FEB)

(Coastal Federal Field, 21st Ave N & Central Pkwy ☎ *843.293.7223 ⊕ mbmarathon.com)* While the main marathon benefits the Leukemia & Lymphoma Society of South Carolina and the Horry County Chapter of the American Red Cross, the one-mile Family Fun Run supports Horry County Schools, and the bike ride raises funds for Horry County Department of Disabilities and Special Needs. This multi-day affair features a 5k race, wheelchair and crank chair race, marathon relay, half-marathon, the full 25-mile marathon, the one-mile Family Fun Run, and a bike course. Advance registration is required; fees vary by event.

Registered runners pick up their packets with information and their racing numbers at the exposition. If the races aren't filled, runners can also register at the Expo. Vendors will also be selling various types of merchandise on these two days. See their website for more information about the races.

MARDI GRAS MYRTLE BEACH FESTIVAL (FEB)

(☎ *843.267.7443)* The Mardi Gras celebration bounces back and forth between February 3 and March 9 depending on what day Easter falls that year. This fun-filled festival tends to ramp up just as the Mardi Gras celebration in New Orleans starts winding down. The festival begins over the weekend with a Cajun cook-

off. There's a masquerade ball on the weekend after. Broadway at the Beach hosts the Mardi Gras Parade and the Mardi Gras Celebration at its Celebrity Square. Coastal Federal Field hosts the Cajun Food Fest.

CANADIAN - AMERICAN DAYS (MAR)

(☎ *843.626.7444)* The weeklong festival marks the beginning of spring with entertainment, exhibits, and food. The festival usually coincides with spring break for Canadian students, the National Shag Dance Championships, and the St. Patrick's Day Parade in North Myrtle Beach. Most events are free and open to the public. The week starts with a kickoff celebration at the Myrtle Beach Convention Center.

The festival has many events, including an antique car show, music performances and shows, a soccer tournament, a reception, nature workshops at the Myrtle Beach State Park and Huntington Beach State Park, fireworks, and food-related exhibits. The Can-Am Little Olympics gives children age three to twelve the opportunity to play various beach games and Wendy's International Kite Fest has participants filling the sky with kites.

Many businesses offer an exchange rate during the festival, so you don't have to go to the bank to convert currency.

The festival spans the Grand Strand, with some events in Myrtle Beach and others in North Myrtle Beach, Surfside Beach, and Murrells Inlet.

RUN TO THE SUN CAR AND TRUCK SHOW (MAR)

(Waccamaw Pottery, 🖰 *peedeestreetrodders.com)* Featuring over 2000 cars and trucks in its exhibition, this is the largest independent car show on the East Coast. The highlight is the "Cruise Down Ocean Boulevard," where all participating vehicles join a parade down the street. The show has door prizes, cash giveaways, and a 50/50 drawing. Safety inspection teams are available to give on-

site inspections for the duration of the show. Proceeds go to benefit the Children's Miracle Network at McLeod Children's Hospital, Christian Rodders Association, Horry Country Sheriff's Department, and to National Multiple Sclerosis Society. The fundraising event takes place at Waccamaw Pottery, located in Waccamaw Factory Shoppes.

THE DOLL SHOW AND SALE (APR)
(Myrtle Beach Convention Center, 2101 N Oak Street ☎ 843.248.5643) The doll show features dolls, as well as accessories, doll-making supplies, fabrics, and lace. Appraisers will be available to look over any dolls. Minor repairs can also be done right at the exhibits. There are raffles to raise money for local charities. This event is sometimes held in March.

GRAND STRAND FISHING RODEO (APR)
(☎ 843.626.7444) The competition begins in April and runs till the end of October. After your fishing trip, enter your catch, regardless of whether it was caught from the pier, the surf, in the inlet or in the deep sea. The entry cards are submitted at official weighing stations in the Grand Strand area. There are monthly drawings for prizes (cash and merchandise), decals, and shoulder patches. At the end of the Rodeo in October, a drawing awards the grand prize of $2,000. The weigh master named on the grand prizewinner's entry receives $200.

THE VETERANS GOLF CLASSIC (MAY)
(3420 Pampas Dr ☎ 843.477.8833 ⁁ veteransclassic.com) To participate in the three-day tournament, at least one team member must be a military veteran or an active member of the military. Individuals are welcome to sign up; they will be paired up with a team before the start of competition.

The three-day tournament has two-person teams playing Best Ball golf on the first day, Texas Scramble on the second day, and Combined Team golf on the final day. Teams will be sorted into groups of roughly 63 teams and can be made up of male or female members or couples.

SUN FUN FESTIVAL (JUN)
(☎ *843.626.7444* 🖰 *sunfunfestival.com*) The city kicks off its summer season with its biggest summer event. The festival is packed with contests, sporting events, and parades. Two beauty pageants crown a Miss Sun Fun and a Miss Bikini Wahine during the festival. The event also includes an air show, sandcastle building, jet ski stunt shows, musical concerts, and beach games. There are beach tennis and volleyball competitions, a 5K run, bocce ball, horseshoe, and watermelon eating contests.

Between 1987 and 1991, Myrtle Beach and Long Beach (Washington) engaged in a rivalry over who could build the longer sand sculpture. Myrtle Beach built its castles during this festival. In 1990, the finished sand castle extended 10.45 miles. In 1991, the 16.39 mile long sand castle made it into the Guinness Book of World Records as the World's Longest Sand Sculpture.

INDEPENDENCE DAY CELEBRATION (JUL)
(☎ *843.448.7690*) Activities take place all over the Grand Strand. Myrtle Beach has its celebration on Coastal Federal Field and has a fireworks extravaganza, magic fountain shows, and patriotic-themed entertainment.

WORLD AMATEUR GOLF CHAMPIONSHIP (AUG)
(☎ *843.477.8833* 🖰 *worldamgolf.com*) The four-day **PGA TOUR** Superstore World Amateur Handicap Championship is held at about 70 of Myrtle Beach's best courses. Over 5,000 amateur golfers participate, coming from all 50 states and 18 other coun-

tries. Flight winners go on to compete in the final championship round at the Dunes Golf Club. Grouped by handicap, men and women pay an entry fee to play and win cash and prizes. The fee includes four rounds of golf on four different courses, admission to nightly functions at the convention center, and several additional benefits. Entry deadline: Aug. 1.

DICKENS CHRISTMAS SHOW AND FESTIVAL (NOV)
(Myrtle Beach Convention Center, 2101 N. Oak Street ☎ 843.448.9483 ⁻ʘ dickenschristmasshow.com) A Christmas-themed arts and crafts show featuring over 400 booths with vendors garbed in traditional Dickensian costumes. Special holiday teas and historic house tours are also offered during the festival. Tickets are required for adults and children above the age of two. Multi-day passes are also available.

BEACH BALL CLASSIC (DEC)
The classic is a premier high school basketball tournament in the United States. Started in 1981 at Socastee High School as an 8-team local tournament, the classic has grown into a 16 team National tournament. The Beach Ball Classic Holiday Invitational is a 16 team National tournament for girls. The Carolina's Challenge women's college game, featuring the University of South Carolina vs. the University of North Carolina and Coastal Carolina University vs. UNC Wilmington, is held during the Holiday Invitational.

Beaches

The Grand Strand boasts 60 miles of sandy beach as it extends south from near South Carolina's north border, and Myrtle Beach is the largest community in the Strand. **Ocean Boulevard** runs north and south of the city, parallel to the Atlantic Ocean. It's the easternmost paved road before the beach and the ocean, giving visitors easy access onto the sand. Myrtle Beach is entirely a public beach, and despite a lot of hotels on Ocean Boulevard, the sand is open to everyone

There are several piers jutting into the ocean: **The Myrtle Beach State Park Pier** at the southern end of the city**, Second Avenue Pier** on 2nd Avenue North, **14th Avenue Pier** on 14th Avenue N, and **Apache Pier** at the northern end of the city.

Visitors familiar with the Pacific Ocean should not expect the Atlantic Ocean to be as turbulent. The waves are relatively small, except for when a storm or hurricane is approaching. The continental shelf on Eastern United States extends more than 60 miles from the shore, forming a gradual incline into the water. Wave swells rolling into shore start breaking when they hit the shelf; the width of the shelf affects the size of the waves as they travel inland.

GENERAL SAFETY

While the water may look tame, the ocean is still very dangerous. Undertow in this area can be very strong. Swimmers caught in the undertow should do their best to not panic and try to float with the waves, as they will bring you back to shore. Bigger waves than usual usually indicate stronger than usual undertow, so it would be safer to stick to the shallow waves.

If the high waves coincide with a full moon and there's a hurricane or tropical storm brewing in the ocean, riptides occur.

The overflow of water coming into shore travels back to the ocean in a narrow current with considerable force and speed. Telltale signs of rip currents are rough, choppy water that appears deeper and darker than normal with swirling debris, kelp, or sand. The current is often strong enough to carry swimmers out into the open ocean – 80 percent of ocean rescues at Myrtle Beach involve riptides. Swimmers caught in a rip should try not to panic and try to angle their bodies to either swim or float parallel to the shoreline. Waves on either side of the narrow current will push you out of the rip and back to shore.

SUN PROTECTION
Just before venturing out for a day on the sand, remember that the sun is strong enough here at Myrtle Beach that you can turn pink in under an hour – sometimes even in 30 minutes. Even on cloudy or cool days, the sun's harmful rays make it through and can cause bad burn. Even the shade is not always enough protection, since the sun's rays reflect off the sand and the water. Remember to apply sun block or sunscreen at least an hour before venturing out, and remember to reapply it frequently, especially if you are swimming.

LIFEGUARDS
Trained lifeguards, certified in rescue and CPR, are on duty on the beach during the season. They will announce current swimming conditions by posting colored flags: yellow for extra caution, red for no swimming. Try to always go to a lifeguard-protected area of the beach. However, during the off-season, there are no lifeguards on duty so be careful when venturing into the water.

The Myrtle Beach **Beach Patrol** [☏ 843.918.1334 ⌁ cityofmyrtlebeach.com/police/beach.html] is a vital unit within the city's police department, offering law enforcement, drowning prevention, rescuing distressed swimmers, and immediate at-the-scene care for the ill and or injured, every day of the year, 24 hours a day. All Beach Patrol officers are certified ocean lifeguards and certified in CPR, First Aid, and Ocean Rescue.

A FEW BEACH RULES

Swimming is not permitted beyond 50 yards from the beach, or over shoulder depth. Sleeping on the beach is prohibited at night Littering on the beach and in the water is against the law. It is illegal to walk on sand dunes to pick or damage sea oats, beach grass, or sand fencing. Be smart. Don't try to bait, fish for, or attract sharks within a half-mile of the beach. Glass bottles, drinking glass, or other glass containers are prohibited on the beach by law. Alcohol is prohibited on the beach – both consumption and possession. Open containers with alcohol are not allowed on the beach or any other public access area. Fireworks are prohibited within city limits (but legal in South Carolina).

While driving on the beach is not allowed, you can ride horses on the beach after obtaining a permit from the city clerk. If you are bringing a pet, familiarize yourself with the area's pet rules before traveling. All motorized craft must be at least 50 yards beyond bathers; jet skis must be at least 100 yards away. All boats must be registered with a permit secured from a lifeguard. Rafts must be covered with fabric and have ropes attached to their entire perimeters. Conducting business of any kind of the beach, including promotions such as free samples, is prohibited.

WATER RECREATION

Along with sunbathing, playing volleyball or other sports on the sand, or just frolicking in the surf, Myrtle Beach offers a wide range of water activities. While swimming is prohibited beyond

50 yards from shore, visitors can try a variety of water sports, fishing, and boating at both the beaches on the city's east side, and the Intracoastal Waterway on the city's west side.

WATER SPORTS

During their stay, visitors can try water sports, including surfing, Wave Runners, and parasailing. The calmer waters are friendly for novices. Fishing, windsurfing, and boating are also popular pastimes. The Intracoastal Waterway is popular for water skiing and kayaking. Local marinas often offer equipment rentals.

Scuba diving is not allowed within city limits or near the piers. Divers can opt to go down to Surfside Beach or other parts of the Grand Strand, including North Myrtle Beach and Murrells Inlet. Local Myrtle Beach shops will have the equipment you will need.

SURFING

Myrtle Beach offers beginners a chance to learn surfing under comparatively tame conditions. While the waves may not be exciting enough (unless a storm is approaching) for those used to tall waves, the area supports a fairly active community of surfers.

Surfing is restricted to certain areas and times on the beach. All surfers are required to wear leashes.

Surfboards are not allowed in Myrtle Beach between 9am and 5pm, from March 16 to Sept. 15, except in four locations: 29th Avenue South, 41st Avenue North through 47th Avenue North, 82nd Avenue North to the city limits, and from the south side of 8th Avenue North to the north end of the boardwalk. The area from 8th Avenue North to the boardwalk is actually open only from Oct. 1 to April 15.

WATERSKIING

While most of the visitors focus on the ocean while at Myrtle Beach, the Intracoastal Waterway on the city's west side also offers a variety of opportunities for water sports. The calmer waters encourage water skiing.

In South Carolina, water skiing is prohibited between sunset and sunrise. State law also considers it a three-person operation: the boat operator, an observer, and the skier. The boat operator is responsible for navigating the boat, monitoring the speed, and watching the skiers in order to adjust the speed to match their abilities. The observer must be at least 12 years old and must keep a constant eye on the skier, the tow rope, and the boat's wake. The skier is responsible for wearing a ski belt or personal flotation device the entire time and communicating any problems with the operator and the observer.

WATER RENTALS AND ACTIVITIES

Visitors will quickly notice a wide array of shops offering equipment rentals, sales, and more for many diverse water-related activities.

SURF CITY
(3001 North King Hwy ☎ 843.626.7919) Surf City sells and rents surfboards, body boards, skateboards, and related equipment, including wet suits, booties, gloves, hoods, and swimwear.

THE SAIL & SKI CONNECTION
(515B US 501 ☎ 843 626.7245) The Sail & Ski Connection sells a wide variety of boating gear and offers kayak rentals and tours, plus water skiing and wet suits. A single kayak with life jacket and

paddle goes for $25 and a tandem one for $30. Upon request, the outlet will deliver the kayak to wherever you are staying. Call first to inquire about delivery, fees, and pricing.

While there are weekly (supervised) kayak tours along the salt marshes at nearby Murrells Inlet, the outfitter will accommodate specific location requests around Myrtle Beach. The salt marsh trips costs around $40 per person and lasts three hours. Along with kayak rentals and tours, the store provides waterskiing equipment and wet suits. (Seasonal)

DOWNWIND SAILS
(2915 South Ocean Blvd ☎ 843.448.7245) Right on the beach, Downwind Sails offers rentals, rides, and lessons for bananas, jet skis, and parasails. Prices vary on equipment, time of the year, and availability. The location rents out sailboats and Hobie Cats (see: Boating). Regular beach volleyball tournaments are also held at this location. Everything is significantly discounted after August, as the heavy tourist season winds down. (Seasonal)

MYRTLE BEACH WATER SPORTS
(Multiple locations, one is at 5835 Dick Pond Rd ☎ 843.497.8848 ⊕ myrtlebeachwatersports.com) This location rents out jet skis, jet boats, and pontoons by the hour. Parasailing, island tours and dolphin watches are also available. Specials on rentals and tours are offered throughout the year, so be sure to inquire about discounts. (Seasonal)

X-TREME SURF & SKATEBOARD COMPANY
(515 Hwy 501 ☎ 843.626.2262) Locally owned, X-treme sells clothing apparel as well as equipment and accessories for surfers and skateboarders. The staff is also willing to answer questions such as possible surfing locations.

OCEAN WATERSPORTS
(405 S Ocean Blvd ☎ 843.445.7777 ⌂ parasailmyrtlebeach.com) Located between the Family Kingdom and the Holiday Inn, the shop offers parasailing, banana boat rides, and ocean kayak rentals. The company uses diesel powered Premium Parasail Winch Boats for parasailing. The boat carries six fliers and up to a maximum of six non-flying observers per trip. A photo service takes pictures (12 photos on a roll) of the parasailing experience.

Tandem and triple flights are available for anyone not interested in a solo flight or weigh less than the weight minimum - 100 pounds. Para sailors are on the boat for less than an hour.

ADVENTURE WATER SPORTS
(3901 Hwy 544 Unit-C ☎ 843.444.2969) This family-oriented business provides jet ski rentals, sports boats, kayaks, and other equipment. Boat rentals are for either a half-day or a full day. Single and double kayaks are available for rental. A credit card deposit is required for all jet ski rentals and sports boats. The outfitter is open daily.

HAGUE MARINA
(#1 Hague Dr, off SC 707 at the Intracoastal Waterway ☎ 843.293.2141) George Russ manages the Hague and offers yacht service, supplies, and storage – wet, dry, covered, uncovered. Transient dockage runs to $1 per foot per night. Water and electric hookups plus a ship's store are onsite. The Hague is open from 8am to 6pm everyday from spring through fall, and from 8am to 5:30pm in the winter.

OSPREY MARINA
(8400 Osprey Rd ☎ 843.215.5353 ⌂ ospreymarina.com) Located next to the Waccatee Zoo, the Osprey opened in January 1997. All 96 slips are rented by the year, and offers dry storage, cable

TV, phone, water, and 30- and 50-amp electric hookups. The marina provides a pump out station as well as gasoline and diesel fuels. Showers, laundry facilities, and an onsite convenience store is available. The marina is open from 8am to 6pm.

DOWNWIND SAILS
(2915 South Ocean Sails Blvd ☎ *843.448.7245)* Right on the beach, Downwind Sails rents out 14- and 16-foot sailboats and Hobie Cats for about $35 per hour. Lessons are also available for novices, and highly recommended, for $45 per hour. The location offers rentals, rides, and lessons for bananas, jet skis, and parasails (see: Water Sports). Prices vary on equipment, time of the year, and availability. Regular beach volleyball tournaments are also held at this location. Everything is significantly discounted after August, as the heavy tourist season winds down. (Seasonal)

BOATING

Boating is a fun way to spend some time on the water, whether it is part of a fishing expedition or just lazily floating down the Intracoastal Waterway. However, boating is not recommended if the water is choppy, if the wind shifts, or if lightning is visible since it is a sign of an approaching storm.

While cruising, change seats carefully, especially in small crafts, to avoid capsizing the vessel. Stay low and near the center line. Be careful when passing a powerboat, and anchor from the bow with a line that is at least five times as long as the water's depth.

While anyone at least 16 years old can legally pilot a boat in South Carolina, every year there are too many deaths caused by young, reckless or drunk watercraft operators in accidents. So use your common sense. Give large ships with restricted maneuverability the right of way, stay away from docks, piers, and swimming areas, and take responsibility for damage caused by your wake. Observe safety regulations and do not try to operate any water-sports equipment unless you've been trained.

Individuals younger than 16 wanting to pilot a boat must complete a boater education course and pass a test. The courses are offered through the US Coast Guard Auxiliary, US Power Squadron, and the Department of Motor Vehicles. The DMV also offers educational handbooks to study prior to the test.

BASIC BOATING RULES
When approaching another boat in open water, each party must move to the right after a short (one second) horn signal and an answering signal from the other vessel. If crossing paths, the boat to the right has the right of way. Sound one short blast to indicate that you are altering course to starboard, or two short blasts to indicate you are heading port, or three short blasts to indicate you are heading to stern so that the other vessel knows and can act accordingly.

In all situations, the boat being overtaken has right-of-way, even if the overtaking ship enters the danger zone. The overtaking boat must sound two long and one short blasts if it intends to pass on the right, and two long, two short blasts if passing on the left. If you are being overtaken, respond with one long, one short, one long, and one short, to indicate that you understand and agree with the action.

When leaving the dock, you have no right of way until you are completely clear. It is your responsibility to leave port without endangering others, and it's a good idea to sound one long blast just before departing. All sailboats under sail and no motor and fishing boats have right of way and should be given a wide berth, except when a sailboat is overtaking a motorboat. The motorboat then maintains right-of-way.

In boats less than 16 feet in length, each person must have a wearable life vest aboard. If the boat is more than 16 feet in length, a ring buoy or other safety device that can be thrown must be aboard the vessel in addition to a wearable life vest for each passenger. All children younger than age 12 on a vessel less than 16 feet in length are required to wear the life jacket while aboard.

Before casting off, always check the vessel for a portable radio to check weather reports, a flashlight and extra batteries, matches, a navigation map of the area, suntan lotion, a first-aid kit, sunglasses, a raincoat, and an extra length of tie-line. Tell someone where you're going, who is going to be on board, and how long you will be way. Before starting the engine, open hatches, run the blower, and sniff for gasoline fumes in the engine and fuel areas. Make sure all gear is packed.

By South Carolina law, an operator of any vessel must file a written report with the authorities in case of an accident, including but not limited to, damages to the vessel or equipment, injury or loss of life, and missing passengers. Grounding, capsizing, someone falling overboard, collision, sinking, striking another boat or a propeller, swamping, flooding, fire, an explosion, or the disappearance of a craft must also be reported.

You can file a verbal report or request a form by calling the **U.S. Coast Guard Boating Safety Hotline** at 800.368.5646. While injury or death of an individual must be reported within 48 hours of the incident, damage to a vessel or property can be reported within 10 days.

If you own your own sailing vessel, you can store them in the local marina, most of which are open year-round. Don't have a boat, but would like to captain one? Looking for a pontoon boat to spend a leisurely day? The area marinas rent out watercraft during the summer, before Labor Day.

FISHING

While mosquitoes and the heat make fishing a challenge in the summer, there are plenty of fishing opportunities at Myrtle Beach for serious hobbyists and beginners picking up a pole for the first time. The piers are popular fishing spots in Myrtle Beach, and each pier has its own weighing station.

You can also rent a boat to go inshore or offshore fishing – most fishing charter boats leave from North or South Strand. It's customary to tip a guide or charter mate on your fishing expedition about the same as you would tip in a restaurant – about 15 to 20 percent of your total bill. If you are going to be fishing without a local captain or guide, check on current regulations before embarking on your fishing trip. Fines for illegal fishing can be substantial.

Newcomers to deep-sea fishing should take seasick medication the night before the trip. Most of the local pharmacies carry over the counter motion-sickness medication as well as patches to affix behind the ear. Once an expedition leaves the dock, it will not return to the shore early just for seasick passengers. If you plan to buy waders or boots, always buy them one and a half sizes larger than your shoe size so that you can slip them off in case you fall overboard.

SURF FISHING

The easiest way is "surf" fishing. This kind of fishing is popular during the less humid months in autumn and is best during low tide (check the tide tables before heading out!). Washed-out areas along the shoreline that resemble creek beds in the sand are ideal, such as a slough, pool, or a drop-off, because they are often two feet or more deeper than its surroundings. Surf fishermen (and women!) can be spotted up and down the shore, armed with a simple tackle rig and a bucket for bait and catch. The catch includes bluefish, flounder, whiting, spot, pompano, and channel bass. Pompano, abundant in the late summer, swim in the surf zone, right where the waves break on the beach, and feast on tiny mole crabs before they burrow into the sand. Whiting, also caught in the summer, are usually found around groins, sloughs and cuts along open beaches.

INSHORE FISHING
Inshore fishing gives avid anglers the opportunity to hook larger fish including the crevalle jack, Florida pompano, sheepshead, Southern flounder, black drum, spotted sea trout, king mackerel, Spanish mackerel, red drum, and whiting. Spotted sea trout is found in lower estuaries in the summer and around oyster bars, rocks, and pilings in the spring and fall. The recreational size limit for the sea trout is 13 inches, and only 10 can be kept per day. While red drum can be found in the main estuaries in July, they are usually smaller than the state's minimum size requirements – 14 inches. Red drum grows to between 20 and 30 pounds by late summer and can be found around jetties and at the mouths of the bays and sounds. Five red drums a day is the legal limit. South Carolina law prohibits "gigging" red drum or spotted sea trout from December through February. Flounder gigging is permitted in the summer, especially aboard shallow-draft boats. Flounder must be at least 12 inches long and only 20 can be kept per day. The crevalle jack is considered the toughest fish to catch in the area, lurking in the dark around rips during ebb tide. Jacks should be released.

OFFSHORE FISHING
Offshore fishing trips give you the opportunity to fish sea bass along underwater reefs, blue marlin through the Gulf Stream, yellow fin tuna, barracuda, crevalle jack, wahoo, fish called dolphin, king mackerel, little tunny, Spanish mackerel, white marlin,

amberjack, and sailfish. In the summer, often after four or five consecutive days of flat, calm conditions, many of the bluewater fish move to within 15 miles of the coast. In the early spring, that changes to nearly 50 miles offshore to catch the same fish. Heat drives most of the fish down to the deeper cooler waters, so early morning and late afternoon are when the fish are really biting as they are in a feeding frenzy.

Blue marlin in the area tend to be about 125 to 200 pounds, below the 99-inch minimum fork length. Marlin fishing is the most productive in ocean depths of 300 to 1200 feet in the summer, and 80 feet in cooler weather. Sailfish are abundant during July and August, but may be caught only 10 miles off the beach. Unfortunately, many are also below the minimum 63 inch fork length. Averaging 35 to 45 pounds, they are often found in weed lines, current rips, and natural reefs in 120 to 300 feet of water.

Dolphin and wahoo sizes decline over the summer: dolphin drops from 10 to 20 pounds to about 8 pounds, wahoo starts at 35 to 50 pounds and drops to 20 pounds by the end of the season. They are best fished at 180 to 600 feet. Yellowfin tuna are also found at this depth, although they grow on average to 45 pounds during the summer.

Amberjack and barracuda are also possible offshore fishing targets and most are also catch-and-release. King mackerel frequent artificial and natural reefs. For the most part, the mackerel in the area tend to stop biting after 10 am in the summer. The female mackerel can be found near shore just outside of bays and sounds while the males are typically in depths of 60 to 120 feet. Little tunny, locally known as bonito, crevalle jack and Spanish mackerel, can be fished 15 miles offshore during the summer as well as one to five miles outside bays, sounds, and artificial reefs. Flocks of wheeling and diving tern as the birds feed on fish parts as the fish feed indicate where the schools are.

OYSTERS AND CLAMS

Harvesting oysters and clams are not typically a Myrtle Beach activity – but are available in other parts of the Grand Strand. For those interested in shrimping, the area is the home of two species: brown and white shrimp. Brown shrimp are harvested beginning from June. Harvesting for white shrimp start late July and early August; the white shrimp disappear from creeks by late October. Shrimp are harvested by seines, cast nets, and drop nets. The best time for harvesting using nets is during the fall as the shrimp migrates towards the ocean, especially during falling tide. The legal daily limit is 48 quarts with heads attached, or 29 quarts with heads off per boat or seining party.

Seines cannot exceed 40 feet in length, and the webbing must be a half-inch square mesh or larger for nylon nets. State law prohibits blocking more than half of width of the slough or creek with the nets. The nets also must be pulled by hand – not dragged by a motorized boat or staked in place with poles. Cast nets which are cheaper and less cumbersome than seines, have no size restrictions and are most effective during low tide. Casting in deeper areas – three to four feet – during the day will catch larger shrimp since they flee from the light. Please note that the law limits cast net harvesting to the 60 days between Sept. 1 and Nov. 15. Drop nets can be fished from bridges, docks, or seawalls, and are almost exclusively used at night.

CRABBING

Another option is to go crabbing. South Carolina law allows two crab pots to each individual without a license, as long as the pots are clearly marked with the owner's name. If its point-to-point width is less than five inches, or if the female is carrying an egg mass, the crab must be released. Leave the pots in water deep enough that they will not be exposed during low tide, or the crabs will die. Many people use drop nets and collapsible traps from docks and bridges, as well as a long-handled dip net, several yards of string, and bait.

Crabs are generally inactive when water temperatures fall below 55°F in the winter. The period between October and December is the best time to harvest large mature crabs. Always keep crabs alive, and cool, such as a cooler with some ice. The crabs will die from lack of oxygen in a container full of water.

PLACES TO FISH

Don't just drop your fishing line into any body of water and hope to score a catch. Myrtle Beach has a selection of locations specifically for the fishing enthusiast.

APACHE PIER
(Apache Campground, 9700 Kings Rd ☎ 843.497.6486 ⌐ apachefamilycampground.com) Measuring 1220 feet in length, the Apache Pier claims to be the longest pier on the East Coast. There is a bait-and-tackle shop, arcade, restaurant, and aquarium filled with indigenous fish, right on the pier. The pier features nightly entertainment from May 30 to Labor Day. The pier charges a fee whether you want to wish or only watch (campers staying on-property get a discount). Fishing hours are reduced in the winter.

MYRTLE BEACH STATE PARK
(4401 South Kings Hwy ☎ 843.238.5326 ⌐ discoversouthcarolina.com) The park charges a $2 fee to enter the park, except from Nov. 5 to mid-March. Regular admission cost is $4.50 per fishing pole. Season passes are available. Fishing rods are available for rental at $4 a piece, and pier is open as long as the park is – from 6am to 10pm every day. There's also a tackle, bait, ice, and a gift shop.

PIER 14 RESTAURANT, LOUNGE AND FISHING PIER
(1306 North Ocean Blvd ☎ 843.448.4314) More popular as a restaurant, Pier 14 however conducts its fishing business through its gift and tackle shop. To fish costs $6, to watch is free. An arcade and an outdoor patio are open to the public. Pier 14 is accessible from 7am to midnight all summer and fall, until November. The pier is closed in the winter, from November to February.

SECOND AVENUE PIER AND RESTAURANT
(200 North Ocean Blvd ☎ 843.626.8480) The 905 feet long pier is lighted, and has a T-shape end. The pier is open from 7am to 11pm from March 1 to early October. A fishing pass to fish off the pier costs $6 a day, to watch, $1. Season passes are also available. The tackle shop offers a full line of bait, tackle, rods, and reels. Along with the stop, the pier boasts a gift shop, arcade, and a full-service restaurant.

SPRINGMAID PIER
(3200 South Ocean Blvd ☎ 843.238.5189, x3008) Bait and ice are sold here. Tackle can be bought or rented. Admission is $6.50 per person to fish, and spectators can watch for free. There are special weekly and year round rates offered. The pier is open seven days a week from 6am to midnight year-round. The tackle shop has limited off-season hours.

CITY BAIT & TACKLE
(713 Eighth Avenue N and Alder St ☎ 843.448.2543) This family business keeps a steady supply of mullet, shrimp and squid for bait, and a wide range of tackle. Questions about suggested casting locations? This is the place to ask.

*The **Pavilion** amusement park, one of Myrtle Beach's top attractions, closed its doors in 2006.*

Golf

Visitors came to Myrtle Beach primarily during the summer. Golf, however, has stretched the city's busy season into the spring and fall, as visitors found the weather ideal for playing conditions during those months.

Course Greens Fees:

$	=	< $60
$$	=	$60 - $90
$$$	=	$91 - $120
$$$$	=	$121 - 190
$$$$$	=	> $190

Golf is a serious business here in Myrtle Beach.

A popular golf destination, there are tournaments, golf packages, and golf schools available. Most courses arrange package deals with area hotels and advertising groups. These packages usually include a welcome gift, breakfast, fees to play on the course, and a golf cart. Hotels usually can arrange for deep discounts on greens fees, so check with your hotel before calling courses directly to schedule tee times.

Since the subtropical climate makes outdoor activities pleasant almost every day, bargains for golf can be found even out of season in the summer and winter. The heavy golf discounts during the summer often balance out the inflated hotel rates. As the summer crowds thin out, some courses adjust their fees, charging less for afternoon tee times than for mornings.

In recent years, the soaring real estate prices have made it harder for golf courses to remain open. With Myrtle Beach developing rapidly and new buildings being constructed everyday, many of the independent golf courses have either closed down completely, or closed down portions of the course to make room for housing components.

GOLF INFO AND ORGANIZATIONS

For those wishing to plan a golf vacation in America's golf paradise, the following places will provide some information on getting to the greens.

MYRTLE BEACH GOLF HOLIDAY
(☎ 800.845.4653 ⌨ golfholiday.com) A nonprofit association made up of 77 area accommodations, 72 golf courses and 4 golf schools, Myrtle Beach Golf Holiday represents the area from Georgetown, South Carolina, to Southport, North Carolina. Founded in 1967, the organization helps visitors plan and reserve golf vacations. The group provides a vacation planner with information on resorts and golf courses for free, upon request. The planner is also full of travel tips and how to directly book a golf vacation.

The group hosts the Palmetto High School Golf Championships each year. Each spring, Golf Holiday manages the Hootie and the Blowfish Monday After The Masters Celebrity Pro-Am Golf Tournament and Golfapalooza in North Myrtle Beach. The group also manages the Summer Family Golf Tournaments, the Veterans Golf Classic and the FDNY 9-11 Memorial Golf Outing.

CLASSICS OF MYRTLE BEACH
(⌨ myrtlebeachclassics.com) An umbrella organization that represents some of the area's top courses and resorts, the group offers vacation packages that include extra amenities such as fine restaurants, exercise and relaxation facilities, and entertainment. The group arranges everything: you just pick the resort, courses, and tee times.

PRIME TIMES GOLF & TRAVEL

(Baggage Claim, Myrtle Beach International Airport ☎ 843.443.6000) Prime Times offer daily and weekly golf club rentals right at the airport. Instead of losing the golf clubs during travel, or having them damaged, Prime Times give players the option of renting a set after they arrive to Myrtle Beach. Shoe rentals are available. Golf accessories and apparel can be bought here.

Golfers can schedule tee times on area courses, reserve/confirm lodging, and make dinner reservations while at the office. ($50 for one-two day rentals; $99 for three-four days; a fee of $25 per day applies for each additional day)

BURROUGHS & CHAPIN GOLF MANAGEMENT

(☎ 866.772.4669) The management company owns or operates several golf courses in the Grand Strand and at least three in Myrtle Beach. Golfers can call the company to schedule tee times.

TOURNAMENTS

Interested in learning about – or participating in – one of the area's tournaments? The following organizations may be able to help.

PGA TOUR SUPERSTORE WORLD AMATEUR HANDICAP CHAMPIONSHIP

(☎ 800.833.8798) This tournament used to be known as the DuPont Coolmax World Amateur Handicap Championship until the name was changed in 2005. The tournament features play at over 75 local golf courses. This matched-handicap competition is one of the oldest and biggest golfing events in the area.

The amateur contest draws well over 5,000 golfers from around the world each year to compete for the title of "World

Champion" and $400,000 in prizes. The prizes include a gift bag, trophies, top-10 prizes in each flight, and random drawings for exotic trips, golf clubs, and golf memorabilia. There are special prizes for lowest net, longest drive, closest to the pin, and holes-in-one.

There's a "World's Largest 19th Hole" party every night during the tournament at the Myrtle Beach Convention Center. Past parties served crab soup, turkeys, hams, roast pig, lasagna and cobbler.

Golfers play four rounds on four different courses over the course of four days, with winners from each "flight" competing in the championship round on the fifth day at the Tournament Player's Club of Myrtle Beach. To make the tournament even more competitive, Myrtle Beach Golf Holiday created six divisions within the tournament field: men (49 and under), senior men (50-59), mid senior men (60-69), super senior men (70 and over), women (49 & under) and senior women (50 and over).

THE NATIONAL RETIRED MILITARY GOLF CLASSIC
(PO Box 3608 ☎ 843.448.2308) The five-day tournament has men playing at Myrtle Beach National and Long Bay, and women at Aberdeen. The entry fee includes golf, cart, awards, prizes, and special drawings. Players receive a Classic Golf shirt and hats for men, visors for women.

The first day of the tournament has a cocktail reception "Ice Breaker" at a local hotel, and scheduled entertainment in the evening after the second day.

Golfers play in ABCD teams for four days. Each day, the foursomes and courses are rotated. Some of the prizes are golf bags, clubs and balls, high value gift certificates, and golf vacations for two. There are par 3 prizes every day and cars for Hole-In-One.

THE VETERANS GOLF CLASSIC

(3420 Pampas Dr ☎ 843.477.8833 ✆ veteransclassic.com) To participate in the tournament, at least one team member must be a military veteran or an active member of the military. Individuals are welcome to sign up; they will be paired up with a team prior to the start of competition.

The three-day tournament has two-person teams playing Best Ball golf on the first day, Texas Scramble on the second day, and a Combined Team golf on the final day. Teams will be flighted into groups of roughly 63 teams based on the team's handicap.

The entry fee covers three rounds of tournament golf, including green fees, cart fees, and the range. Players will attend a welcome reception the evening before the tournament starts and an awards banquet at the end of the tournament. Each player can bring a guest. They will receive a Veteran's Golf Classic logo hat and Veteran's Golf Classic logo golf shirt. The top seven teams in each flight receive a trophy and a gift card to Martin's PGA TOUR Superstore. There are daily contest prizes in each flight. The tournament uses the USGA Slope Handicap System.

Each team plays on three courses. Of the fifteen participating courses, six are located in Myrtle Beach: Man O' War, Myrtle Beach National's West Course and Southcreek, Myrtlewood Golf Club's Palmetto Course, Whispering Pines, and The Wizard. The others are in surrounding communities and are: Angels Trace Golf Links South in South Brunswick Isles, River Hills in Little River, Indian Wells in Surfside, Lion's Paw Golf Links in Ocean Isle Beach, Long Bay Club in Longs, Sandpiper BayGolf & Country Club in Sunset Beach, Sea Trail in Sunset Beach, Shaftesbury Glen Golf & Fish Club in North Myrtle Beach, and Wachesaw East in Murrells Inlet.

SUMMER FAMILY GOLF TOURNAMENT
(3420 Pampas Dr ☎ 800.833.8798 ⌁ summerfamilygolf.com) These are single-day tournaments open for beginner and scratch golfers, regardless of age. The format is two person teams and Captain's Choice. The tournament has three divisions: Open, Couples and Adult/Youth. Individuals will be paired with a tournament before the start of the tournament.

Juniors, 16 years of age and below will play for free at each tournament with a paying adult. The entry fee includes green fees, cart and the chance to win one of many tournament prizes, such as closest-to-the-pin and long drive contests.

Various courses participate in hosting the single-day tournaments throughout the summer, including Myrtle Beach National's South Creek and King's North, Myrtlewood's Palmetto and Pinehills, Pine Lakes, and Grande Dunes.

GOLF COURSES

If you're interested in the courses themselves, following are a few of the more than 100+ courses in the Myrtle Beach and Grand Strand areas. For additional courses, see one of the "Golf Info and Organizations."

ARCADIAN SHORES GOLF CLUB
(Myrtle Beach Hilton, 701 Hilton Rd ☎ 843.449.5217) Rees Jones designed this course, which features standard Bermuda-grass fairways and bent-grass greens. The 6,446-yard par-72 course has more than 60 sand bunkers and several natural lakes. ($$, no walking)

ARROWHEAD COUNTRY CLUB
(1201 Burcale Rd ☎ 843.236.3243 ⌁ arrowheadcc.com) Raymond Floyd designed this 27-hole par-72 course. Each 9-hole course

has its own name. One of them, the 3,119-yard Lakes Course, features a pine forest, fairways, white sand bunkers, and lakes. The 3,123-yard Cypress Course is set amid hardwoods. And the 3,060-yard Waterway Course stretches to the Intracoastal Waterway, passing through hardwoods, mounds, and lakes along the way.

Along with a clubhouse, the club offers a practice facility and a full-stocked pro shop. (summer: $, no walking)

BELLE TERRE GOLF COURSE

(4073 Belle Terre Golf Course Blvd, US 501 ☎ *843.236.8888)* French for "beautiful earth," Rees Jones designed this 54-hole complex. The course features the 3,200-yard, 18-hole Skins Course, a par-58 course. It allows players to either walk or ride along the concrete paths. The course has four par-4s and 14 par-3s, as well as water hazards and bunkers. The 72-par Championship Course measures 7,013 yards from the tees.

Belle Terre's Championship course has played host to numerous events of note including: The Powerbilt Tour's East Coast Championship, The DuPont World Amateur Handicap Championship, The Golf Channel's Drive, Chip and Putt Contest, The Toyota Skills Challenge and Slazenger's National Father & Son Team Classic.

The clubhouse has a pro shop, restaurant, and dressing rooms with showers and lockers. (Skins: $ walk/cart; Championship: $$ no walking)

DUNES GOLF AND BEACH CLUB

(9000 North Ocean Blvd ☎ *843.449.5914* ✆ *dunesgolfandbeachclub.com)* Designed in 1948 by Robert Trent Jones Sr., this is one of the area's oldest courses – the second course built in Myrtle Beach. It's one of the most exclusive private clubs, and is available only to guests staying at the following hotels: the Breakers,

the Caravelle, the Caribbean, the Driftwood, the Dunes Village, and the South Wind. The hotels schedule the tee times. The club has hosted the Senior Tour Championship.

The par-72, 6,174-yard course has PennLink bent-grass greens, wide-open fairways, deep bunkers, and elevated greens. You will play through live oaks and rolling coastal terrain, all while listening to the roar of the ocean in background. Many of the greens are fronted by large, penal bunkers.

The club is famous for its 13th hole, known as the Waterloo. So few people have reached the 13th green in two shots that those who have are immortalized in the club's history books. The club features a grill and a dining room with a panoramic view of the beach. ($$$$)

GRANDE DUNES GOLF COURSE MUST SEE

(1580 Terra Verde Dr ☎ 843.913.1341 ✆ grandedunes.com) Grande Dunes Golf course is set on a bluff overlooking the Intracoastal Waterway, offering panoramic views of the waters and maritime forest. Designed by Roger Rulewich, a senior designer for Robert Trent Jones, the course has numerous elevation changes, wide Bermuda-grass fairways, L-93 bent grass greens, and acres of lakes. Water is part of the play at almost every hole.

The club also features a golf academy with several types of golf-instruction. Schools can be as short as a "lesson, lunch, and golf" or even half a day. Academy participants get a personalized DVD, video analysis of their game, a tips workbook, discount on greens fees, and unlimited number of range balls for the day.

THE LEGENDS COMPLEX

(1500 Legends Dr, off US 501 ☎ 843.236.9318 ✆ legendsgolf.com) Legends Complex has three distinctive courses: Parkland, Heathland, and Moorland. None of the courses in this par-72 6425-yard complex are recommended for beginners. Professionals

have compared the Parkland course to New Jersey's Pine Valley Course in level of difficulty.

Measuring 6190 yards, Heathland has no trees, strong winds, and rolling fairways. The pot bunkers look worse than they really are. Tom Doak designed this course. At 6,125 yards, the par-72 Moorland is downright difficult, including a short par 4 called "Hell's Half Acre." Players with a high handicap are more likely to enjoy play on this P.B. Dye course.

The clubhouse sits in the middle of a green lawn and features an upscale pro shop, a pub, and a dining room. A driving range with greens and flags as targets is also available. ($, no walking)

MAN O'WAR

(5601 Leeshire Boulevard, off US 501 ☎ *843.236.8000* ⏱ *manowargolfcourse.com)* Dan Maples created the course from a 80-acre lake. The 6402-yard par-72 course features a pair of back-to-back island greens, an island 9th hole surrounded by water from tee to green, distinctive wide fairways, and Bentgrass greens. The marina clubhouse also has a practice range. ($$$, no walking)

MYRTLE BEACH NATIONAL

(4900 National Dr, off US 501 ☎ *843.448.2308* ⏱ *mbn.com)* Frank Duane designed all three par-72 courses, with rolling fairways, pine trees, and lakes. The oldest one, the 6413-yard North Course, has Bermuda-grass. It is famous for its par-3 12th hole, which includes sand traps shaped like the letters "SC," bulkheads, and a footbridge. There are over forty bunkers on No. 18.

All juniors age 16 and under play free on both courses as long as they are accompanied by a paying adult. The play-free also extends to courses at several other clubs.

The 6113-yard West Course is a classic Arnold Palmer design, winding through a forest of pines. The regular tees are easy and accessible for all golfers. The back tees are more challenging, featuring numerous doglegs, fairway bunkers and natural hazards.

The Southcreek course measures 6089 yards and is also a Palmer design. The course winds through wetlands and hardwood forests and features guarded Bentgrass greens and numerous waste areas. It is distinctly different from the other two courses. (North Course: $$$; South Creek: $; West Course: $; no walking on all three)

MYRTLEWOOD GOLF CLUB
(1500 48th Avenue North Ext ☎ *843.913.4516* ✆ *myrtlewoodgolf.com)* Myrtlewood Golf Club offers two 18-hole courses: the Palmetto Course and the Pine Hills Course. The Palmetto Course is a traditional course, with fairways that gently twist and turn towards large Tidwarf greens. The course ends along the Intracoastal Waterway. The par 3, 17th hole and 18th hole are considered the best holes on the course.

The Pine Hills Course was designed by Arthur Hills and has contoured fairways and undulating greens. Measuring 6,640 yards from the back tees, the fairways are narrow with condos on both sides. The condos detract from the view and make the play a bigger challenge.

PINE LAKES INTERNATIONAL COUNTRY CLUB
(5603 Woodside Dr ☎ *843.449.6459* ✆ *pinelakes.com)* The oldest course in the area, golfers refer to Pine Lake as the "Granddaddy." Originally called the Ocean Forest Club, it was constructed in 1927. The 62-room antebellum club with rocking chairs on the porch gleams at the top of the course, evoking images of bygone eras.

Robert White, the first PGA president, designed the 6176-yard par-71 course with a Scottish flair. The par-3 7th hole is beautiful in the spring, when the azaleas are in bloom.

Along with having starters in authentic Scottish kilts greeting the players, hot chocolate (on cold days) or a cool mimosa (when it's hot) are served on the first tee. Players also receive a cup of Low-country clam chowder at No. 7, and a "crying towel" at the finish. Overall, "Granddaddy" is a challenging course, with bunkers flanking both sides of fairways. ($$$, no walking)

PRESTWICK COUNTRY CLUB

(1001 Links Rd ☎ 843.293.4101 ⌁ prestwickcountryclub.com) Designed in the classic Scottish tradition, Pete and P.B. Dye's $6 million dollar course surrounds a 20 acre freshwater lake. The course features towering Scottish beams, stairway and church pew bunkers, undulating greens, and dramatic elevation changes. Some of the height changes range up to thirty feet. A 20,000 square foot colonial clubhouse borders the lake on the west.

The front nine winds through a pine forest similar to the Harbourtown Golf Course (also designed by Dye). The back nine is less than a quarter mile from the ocean and has a more open layout. Prevailing ocean winds influence play on this part of the course.

Water comes into play at eight different holes. Prestwick has six sets of tees for all kinds of golfers and measures 7058 yards from the Championship tees. ($$)

RIVER OAKS GOLF PLANTATION

(831 River Oaks Dr ☎ 843.236.2222 ⌁ riveroaksgolfplantation.com) The complex has 27 holes of undulating greens, mounded fairways, and large lakes. Some of the courses feature finger-shaped bunkers. The 6314-yard Bear, 6345-yard Fox, and 6425-yard

Otter Courses are all par-72. The course is beautiful, well maintained, and full of wildlife.

Along with practice areas, players can attend the American Golf Academy (on premises) to improve their game. ($ in the summer, no walking)

WATERWAY HILLS

(US 17 N, ☎ *843.449.6488* 🖰 *mbn.com/wtrholes/index.cfm)* An enclosed tram ferries players across the Intracoastal Waterway to reach Waterway Hills, a 27-hole complex set amid woodland and lakes. Robert Trent Jones designed the courses with rolling terrain and a variety of bunkers. The 3080-yard 17-hole Oaks, 3001-yard Lakes, and 2927-yard Ravine, are par-72 courses featuring challenges based on the landscape reflected in its name. The Oaks Course winds through trees and its fairways are lined with large oak trees. The Lakes Course meanders around five bodies of water and features four holes with water hazards. The third hole at Ravine Course is par-5 and has the following hazard: a 60-foot chasm. ($$ for any 18-hole combination, walking in the afternoon)

WHISPERING PINES

(31 Avenue S and Business 17 ☎ *843.918.2305* 🖰 *wpinesgolf.com)* At Whispering Pines you'll find 6771 yards of traditional and classic design. The 200 acre course was designed by Finger, Dye, and Spahn, and feature tree lined fairways, carefully placed lakes, and undulating greens with Bermuda grass.

The course is also a Certified Audubon Cooperative Sanctuary. The Golf Academy provides instruction programs on the practice range. The entrance to the course is at Highway 17 Business and 22nd Avenue South. ($)

WILD WING PLANTATION

(1000 Wild Wing Blvd ☎ 843.347.9464 ⌁ wildwing.com) A multi-course facility, Wild Wing offers computerized golf carts. These computers calculate and display exact yardages from the ball (wherever it lies) to the center of the green. The computers also offer hints, identifying hazards and terrain around you.

Willard Byrd designed the first course, the Wood Stork Course, which measures 6598 yards. The first eight holes of this par-72 course go through wetlands and the remaining holes wind through a pine forest.

Byrd also designed the 6310-yard par-72 Hummingbird Course. While the wetland perimeter consists of love grass and other native grasses, the fairways are of Bermuda-grass. The classic "links style" course has several lakes, open fairways, four set of tees, pot bunkers, and waste areas.

Rees Jones designed the 18-hole par-72 Falcon Course. Measuring 6697 yards, the course has mounting narrow fairways, small greens, two lakes larger than 20 acres, and a 500-yard bunker. Jeff Brauer and Larry Nelson (two-time PGA champion) designed the Avocet Course, with elevated tees and greens, double fairways, grass bunkers, and a double green. The par-72 course covers 6614 yards.

The clubhouse is a 33,000-square-foot facility that houses WishBones, a restaurant. Wild Wings also has a practice green with a 138-yard practice hole, a putting green, and a pro shop. (Wood Stork: $$; Hummingbird: $$; Falcon: $$$; Avocet: $$$$; walking allowed on Falcon)

THE WIZARD GOLF

(4601 Leeshire Blvd ☎ 843.236.9393 ⌁ wizardgolfcourse.com) Dan Maples designed the Scottish-links course with an Old World flavor. The landscape was transformed to offer mountain golf, complete with rock bridges. The rolling hills on both sides of the

fairway at the 13th hole resemble a Scottish countryside. The clubhouse, resembling an old and battle-worn Celtic castle, completes the effect. The course has dramatic elevation changes. The plantings on the berms and mounds include over 800 species of plants, flowers, and ornamental grasses.

Measuring 6206 yards, The Wizard is a par-71 course. ($$, no walking).

Par 3 Courses

If a full-scale professional golf course is not your thing, you may want to consider one of the area's par 3 courses, which offer shorter (and generally easier) games.

CANE PATCH
(72 Avenue N & Kings Hwy ☏ mbeachkeyattractions.com) Open year-round, the driving range is a good place to practice your swing, whether it's early in the morning or at night (the range is lit for nighttime practice in the summer). Clubs and putters are furnished, and buckets filled with golf balls are sold in bundles of 45, 75, or 115.

Can Patch also offers 9-hole or 18-hole play throughout the year for people looking for par-3 courses. The three 9-hole courses measure 698 yards, 682 yards, and 653 yards.

MIDWAY PAR 3 GOLF
(31 Avenue South & Kings Hwy ☎ 843.913.5335) Eighteen of Midway's 27 holes offer championship-feel play and players find a different situation on each tee box. The facility is lighted for night play.

Miniature Golf

While the area offers several golf courses for enthusiasts, colorful, special-effects-filled (or themed) miniature golf courses are abundant as well. Many of them are geared towards children and novices, but some also attract serious golfers. Most of them offer snack bars or cold drink machines. Inquire about all-day play rates; several places allow you to play as long as you want, and then come back later to play some more.

CAPTAIN HOOK'S ADVENTURE GOLF
(2205 North Kings Hwy ☎ 843.913.7851) Two 18-hole courses evoke Never-Never Land with roving pirates, animated crocs, smoking skulls, and secret caverns. The Lost Boys' course is easier than the Hooks' course, which has uphill shots, water holes, and sand traps.

JUNGLE LAGOON
(Fifth Avenue S and Kings Hwy ☎ 843.626.7894 ⌂ junglelagoon.com) There are two 18-hole courses set in this tropical jungle setting. Both courses are packed with uphill shots, fast downhill curves, and angles. Special rates are available for children under five years of age. All-day play is also offered.

JUNGLE SAFARI MINI GOLF
(71st Avenue North & Kings Hwy ☎ 843.315.0311) The jungle safari has players putting through waterfalls and across streams. There are life-sized elephants, giraffes, and other big game on the course.

JURASSIC ADVENTURE GOLF
(2900 South Kings Hwy ☎ 843.913.5333) The two 18-hole courses evoke the prehistoric era with Tyrannosaurus Rex and other di-

nosaurs. There are discounts for children under five years. While all-day play is offered, it ends early. Check your times beforehand.

NASCAR SPEEDPARK CHALLENGE GOLF
(Hwy 17 Bypass & 21st Avenue North ☎ *843 918 8725)* Strap in and play head-to-head golf on two 18-hole miniature courses. A rather odd combination.

PIRATES WATCH
(1500 South Kings Hwy ☎ *843.448.8600)* All 36 holes offer something: waterfalls, pirates, water traps, and lagoons. All day play is available for limited hours. Inquire beforehand.

RAINBOW FALLS
(9850 US 17 ☎ *843.497.2557)* The two courses feature tricky corners, uphill shots, animal caves, and fairy-tale castles. There are 36 holes. Special rates are offered to children under four years of age and groups. All-day play also ends early.

SHIPWRECK ISLAND ADVENTURE GOLF
(3301 South Ocean Blvd ☎ *843.913.5330)* Players start from an island marina and can choose either the Skipper or Captain miniature course. Play goes through streams and waterfall, and the course features fish and whales.

SPYGLASS
(3800 North Kings Highway ☎ *843.626.9309)* The 18-hole course features obstacles such as waterfalls, uphill holes, and pirates. Discounts are available for senior citizens, children, and groups. Ask when all-day play ends.

TREASURE ISLAND
(48th Avenue N ☎ 843.449.4754) The 18-hole course offers discounts for senior citizens, children, and groups. Ask when all-day play ends.

Area Amusements

When you arrive to Myrtle Beach, you can laze on the sands and soak up some sun. You can also play a couple holes on the golf course. You can toss back some drinks and feast on delicious food. And shops try to entice you with low bargain prices. But after a while, you may start looking for something to do. Not to worry! Myrtle Beach boasts a plethora of places to go and things to see. Amusement parks, racetracks, and nature centers – there's something to see for everyone.

Perhaps the most famous Myrtle Beach attraction was the **Pavilion Amusement Park**. Located in the heart of downtown, along Ocean Boulevard, the Pavilion drew crowds for 58 glorious years until it finally closed in September 2006. The Pavilion opened in 1948, charming millions of visitors every year. The rides had names like Siberian Sleigh Ride, Mad Mouse, and HydroSurge. Attendance at the 11-acre amusement park had been declining for the past few years, and the park showed it in streaks of rust or chipped paint on some rides. Some of the Pavilion rides will be resurrected as part of a mini-park in town, possibly as part of another existing park. Local residents believe some of the rides will also move to Hard Rock Park when it opens in 2008. Others will just be scrapped. Property owners Burroughs & Chapin Company (also of Broadway at the Beach) plan to build a new shopping/dining/entertainment complex on the site.

For the sake of simplicity, we've separated out sporting events, museums, and musical venues into distinct chapters. This chapter focuses on various tourist attractions and fun places to spend a couple hours. Like the rest of the city, the attractions listed in this chapter have different admission fees and operating hours during the off-season. Please call ahead for details.

MUSEUMS

Myrtle Beach's "museums" (apply the term loosely) are a wide array of attractions ranging from the historical and artistic to a kind of kitschy walk-though world of oddities. Following are a few of the more popular area museums.

RIPLEY'S BELIEVE IT OR NOT! MUSEUM MUST SEE

(901 North Ocean Blvd ☎ 843.448.2331 🖰 ripleys.com) Explorer and cartoonist Robert Ripley has a bizarre collection of human oddities and artifacts, such as the shrunken heads from Ecuador. There are more than 500 exhibits housed in the two-story museum. This museum is not a traditional museum – most of the exhibits are either reproductions or fantasy. It bills itself as the "strangest place in Myrtle Beach" and the cracked façade outside just adds to the strangeness.

There's a replica of Cleopatra's barge made entirely out of confectioner's sugar and Van Gogh's self-portrait made of jellybeans. There's a spinning ball weighing over 5 tons right outside the main entrance. At the slightest touch, anyone can change the direction of the ball's spin.

Children five years and under are admitted for free. Ripley's is open year round, but hours vary with the season, so it's best to call for hours. The museum is usually open all afternoon till midnight during the summer.

Instead of buying individual tickets, a Ripley's Combo Pass covers the museum, Ripley's Aquarium, Ripley's Haunted Adventure, Ripley's Moving Theater, and Ripley's Super Fun Zone (all listed under Attractions). With the exception of the aquarium, which is located at Broadway at the Beach, all the other Ripley's attractions are at the same location as the museum's Ocean Boulevard location.

THE CHILDREN'S MUSEUM OF SOUTH CAROLINA

(2501 North Kings Hwy ☎ 843.946.9469 ⌨ cmsckids.org) Kids have fun in a variety of exhibits, such as discovering fossils at the Fossil Hunt and sailing the high seas on the U.S.S. Kids Afloat. Other exhibits: Discovery Lab, Circuit Center, Bubble Mania, Magic School Bus, and Fairway Physics. In the CMSC Medical Center exhibit, kids can see what happens inside a hospital.

With over 7000 square feet of interactive displays, the museum combines science with fun for both children and adults. The museum is located across Oak Street from the Convention Center. The museum's hour vary, depending on the season. Annual family memberships are available.

SOUTH CAROLINA HALL OF FAME

(Myrtle Beach Convention Center, 21 Avenue N and Oak St ☎ 843.918.1225 ⌨ mbchamber.com) The Hall of Fame is a display inside the convention center and has exhibits on the state's history. This designated area honors famous South Carolinians with a portrait and a written biography. Admission is free, and the convention center is open during the day from Monday to Friday all throughout the year.

FRANKLIN G. BURROUGHS AND SIMEON B. CHAPIN ART MUSEUM

(3100 S Kings Hwy ☎ 843.238.2510 ⌨ myrtlebeachartmuseum.org) Housed in a two-story building, the art museum features an art gallery, gift shop, and an art education center. The art gallery – 10 galleries with over 3600 square feet of exhibition space, a tea room, and a large seminar room – is housed in the Springmaid Villa, a 1920s beach house. The permanent exhibit is the Waccamaw Arts and Craft Guild Purchase Award Collection 1970 – 1983. Other exhibits showcase local and national artists. The art education center has an art library, studio classrooms, and stor-

age. Watercolor and children's arts classes are held on weekends every month.

AMUSEMENT PARKS, WATER PARKS

Several area amusement parks are available as diversions to families who prefer to spend some time away from the gold courses. These are small, independent facilities with limited amenities but a lot of classic family-oriented fun. They have seasonal schedules; call ahead for hours of operation.

FAMILY KINGDOM
(300 South Ocean Blvd ☎ 843.626.3447 ↻ family-kingdom.com) Built back in the 1960s over what used to be a marsh, the family-friendly amusement park is located in the heart of Myrtle Beach. A miniature locomotive tours the park's perimeter and an indoor arcade occupies the center of the park. At one point, Family Kingdom boasted both the South's largest old-style roller coaster and largest Ferris wheel. The roller coaster had a 62-foot drop and the Ferris wheel measured nearly 100 feet in diameter. Don't worry, there's an antique carousel for anyone not daring enough to try the wheel or the coaster. The park also has a log flume, two go-kart tracks, bumper cars, and an interactive laser ride.

The rides all accept a pre-determined number of tickets. Some rides require more tickets than others, and individual tickets are available for sale. Wristbands are available that allow unlimited access to rides.

Owned today by the Sea Mist hotel, the amusement park also built a separate children's park on the premises: Kiddie Land. A separate area for young children and toddlers, Kiddie Land has a miniature Ferris wheel, a child-sized roller coaster, and other rides designed for small bodies.

The water park is separate from the main park. There are three water flumes, (one with a 185 foot drop), four speed slides, and a 400 square foot Lazy River with waterfalls. Children can enjoy splash pools with two rain trees, a uniquely designed waterfall, and eight kiddie slides.

Both parks provide some additional services to make the visit comfortable and safe. Both the amusement park office and the water park office have staff trained in first aid, or an EMT. The amusement park office also has a lost-and-found. Strollers (both single and double) and wheelchairs are available on a first-come-first-served, at the Parking Lot Booth.

The park prides itself on a family atmosphere. The park reserves the right to deny entry to anyone wearing clothing with offensive words or pictures. Pets, with the exception of guide dogs, are not allowed in the park.

Open from late March to late November, operating hours vary by the season. During the peak season, the park is open from late afternoons to midnight Monday through Friday, and from early afternoon – 1 PM – to midnight on weekends. There are a number of ticket plans. A two-day combo pass is available – giving access to the water park one day, and the amusement park the next day – as well as single-day pass to both parks. The combo pass excludes Go Karts and pony rides. Wristbands are also available for half the cost for second-day admission. The wristbands must be used within seven days of purchase. Visitors with Military ID get discounts. Call ahead to figure out what you want.

NASCAR SPEEDPARK

(1820 21st Ave. N. Ext. ☎ *843.918.8725* ✆ *nascarspeedpark.com)*
The SpeedPark combines the fun of go-karts and the thrill of the NASCAR stock-racing circuit in one attraction. The 26-acre park has seven tracks, two miniature golf courses, an in-

door/outdoor restaurant, some kiddie rides, an arcade, and a souvenir shop selling NASCAR merchandise. Some numbers: the park has 151 downsized race cars, 4000 Goodyear Racing Eagle tires and 17 show cars on display.

If you are interested in racing, you will be able to measure how fast you were driving. The scoring system measures the lap speed of a car with a margin of error of only .001.

Designed to test your skills, each of the seven tracks have varying levels of difficulty. As such, each track has its own driver height requirements. The 200-foot "Qualifier" is great for children, as long as they are at least 40 inches tall. Drivers need to be at least 48 inches tall to drive on the 725-foot "Champions" track. An indoor track, the "Slidewayz" has a 52 inches minimum. Slidewayz is a slick track, in a tight oval with a highly polished surface.

Drivers for the "Family 500" track must be at least 54 inches. However, drivers can take along a passenger on this 1,200-foot track, provided the passenger is at least 40 inches tall. Twenty-five drivers compete against each other on this track, which features both a tunnel and a bridge.

The 800-foot slick track "Intimidator" is for drivers at least 50 inches tall. Twelve open-wheeled cars compete in each race on this track, which takes its name from NASCAR champion Dale "Intimidator" Earnhardt. This short, oval track features high banking.

The other two tracks, considered high-performing, is very challenging for drivers. The requirements mandate the drivers be at least 64 inches tall for these two. Drivers on the "Competitor" track race half-scale NASCAR style cars on a 36-foot wide D-shaped oval with high-banked curves. "Thunder Road" is the fastest and largest track at the park, measuring half-a-mile in length. The cars, 5/8-scale NASCAR Winston Cup-style cars, were custom-built for this twisting and turning road. To drive on

"Thunder Road" drivers need to be at least 16 years old, have a valid state-issued driver's license, *and* be at least 64 inches tall. The driver must also be wearing closed-toe shoes.

If you are not interested in racing, you can try any of the other attractions. The speed bumper boats are double-seat, electric powered boats featuring water shooters. Drivers must be at least 44" tall and passengers at least 40" tall. The Kiddie Speedway has NASCAR themed cars for little ones and their parents. The children must be at least 36 inches tall.

Sky Wheels, a Ferris wheel for kids, allows children at least 36 inches tall to ride alone. Shorter children must be accompanied by an adult. Slick Spin is the teacup ride – and again, children must be at least 36 inches tall to ride alone or they must be accompanied by an adult.

NASCAR Silicon Motor Speedway features 8- percent scale, 750 HP full motion NASCAR race simulators. You must be at least 52 inches to drive, and the passenger must be least four years old and 40 pounds.

MYRTLE WAVES

(3000 10 Avenue N ☎ 843.913.9260 ↻ myrtlewaves.com) This 20-acre water park has more than 30 rides and attractions, making it one of the largest water parks in the area. Over a million gallons of water splash through the rides, with intriguing names such as Snake Mountain, Pipeline Plunge, and Ricochet Rapids. There are two body flume rides and a wave pool. Along with a Lazy River, there's a 256-foot Racin' River that swirls riders around at nearly 10 miles per hour.

The Bubble Bay leisure pool has bubbler jets. The just for kids Tad-pool is 18 inches deep and has a Little Dipper Slide and the Magic Mushroom water fountain.

The park recommends wearing comfortable sandals or aqua shoes and a bathing suit. Shirts are not allowed on flume rides, and eyeglasses may not be worn on slides. The park has food concessions and a picnic area. The park is open weekends from April to May and in September. From late May through August, Myrtle Waves is open from 10 AM to 5 PM. During the peak season, the park extends its closing time to 6 PM.

Admission to Myrtle Waves covers all the water rides for the entire day, life vests (upon request), free parking, complimentary tubes, and showers and changing facilities.

HARD ROCK PARK

(Fantasy Harbor-site near River Oaks Drive, US 501 and Intracoastal Waterway ☏ hrpusa.com) Slated to open April 2008, the $400 million theme park will have over 40 rides and attractions as well as 15,000 seat outdoor amphitheater. The park is tied in with the Hard Rock Café restaurant. The park's "Mount Rockmore," a three-story tall sand sculpture, features the faces of John Lennon, Bob Marley, Elvis Presley, and Jimi Hendrix. The 140-acre park is along the old Air Force base near Myrtle Beach Airport, at the Fantasy Harbor site. Ocean Boulevard Shuttle will provide airport pickup service from Myrtle Beach Airport to Hard Rock Park, the company said.

NATURE

While "nature" is hardly a word to describe many of the attraction of the Grand Strand, there are a few places for visitors to experience some natural (or at least "naturalistic") wonders.

THE CAROLINA SAFARI JEEP TOURS MUST SEE

(606 65 Street N ☎ 843.272.1177) The custom designed jeeps hold ten to fourteen passengers. The tour directors show off natural coastal attractions, historic areas, old plantations, and a

barrier island. Binoculars are provided and you are encouraged to take pictures.

The directors give an overview of area history and tells\ ghost stories of local wandering spirits. The tour includes Atalaya, a Spanish-style castle, the old homes located on Pawleys Island, a maritime forest, marshes, historic grave sites, and nesting bald eagles.

The jeeps have covers for rainy days and heat for chilly days. Pickup from the hotel/resort you are staying at can be arranged. You can also request additional stops on the itinerary.

Tours run year round, seven days a week, and advance reservations are required.

WACCATEE ZOOLOGICAL FARM

(8500 Enterprise Rd ☎ 843.650.8500 ⁃ waccateezoo.com) The zoo houses unusual animals, including the Bengal Tigers, as well as the traditional lions, tigers, bears, and monkeys. The 500-acre center includes pasture and woodlands for zebras, buffalo, and deer. There are over 100 species of animals at the zoo. The walk through the zoo is about a mile long.

The zoo originated as a private collection of exotic and domestic animals. It continues to receive no state or federal funding. Located where the Waccamaw River, Intracoastal Waterway, and Socastee Creek meet, the zoo is a natural wildlife sanctuary and a breeding ground for many species of migratory birds.

Parks and Recreation

Myrtle Beach is blessed with natural beauty – with clean sands, the sparkling Atlantic Ocean, inland woods, and the Intracoastal Waterway, to name just a few. The comfortable climate means sunny days in the summer, breezy autumns, fairly mild winters punctuated with brisk days, and early spring. Visitors can enjoy being outdoors for most of the year.

STATE AND CITY PARKS

This section describes some of the government-operated parks in Myrtle Beach. Along with a variety of parks and recreation centers, Myrtle Beach also offers campsites, picnic shelters, and lodging. To reserve any of them, visit www.southcarolinaparks.com or call 866.345.7275.

MYRTLE BEACH STATE PARK MUST SEE!

(4401 S. Kings Hwy, off US 17 S ☏ 843.238.5325) Located at the south end of the city, Myrtle Beach State Park is a 312-acre oceanfront park. Visitors can get a glimpse of what the region looked like before the developers swarmed in.

Park facilities include over 300 camping sites, which are available on a first-come-first-served basis (40 additional sites can be reserved up to 14 days in advance). The park also offers five cabins, two apartments, picnic areas, playground equipment, and a snack bar. Swimmers can swim in the ocean or in the park's pool. Pets are not allowed.

There's a nature trail and a nature center where a park naturalist conducts activities year-round. The nature center has snakes, turtles, and marine animals. The park also has a birdhouse, a backyard wildlife habitat and a butterfly garden. Fishing for flounder, whiting, spots, Spanish mackerel, and king mackerel is allowed in the park. Pier fishing is allowed off the 730-foot fishing pier. Surf fishing is also allowed.

The Civilian Conservation Corps, a federal agency created by Franklin D. Roosevelt as part of his New Deal program during the Great Depression, built this park in the 1930s. During World War II, the military used the park as a coastal defense staging area. The first publicly accessible state park in South Carolina, it has the first campground and fishing pier in the area. The park's maritime forest is a Heritage Trust Site.

While the park is open year-round from early morning to late night, the office is open only during regular business hours. The entrance fees, already affordably, are heavily discounted in the summer. South Carolina seniors and children between six and 15 years in age have discounted tickets. Children younger than six years old go in for free. "Discover South Carolina's" site www.discovercarolina.com/html/s01overview.html provides curriculum-based social studies programs for South Carolina school children.

CITY PARKS

The city parks are open 24 hours a day and have no entrance fees. For questions about the parks, call the recreation department at 843.918.2280.

The city of Myrtle Beach maintains public residential parks. There are two in the north end of the city - Gray Park (45 Avenue N and Burchap Drive) and McLeod Park (61 Avenue N) – and two along Ocean Boulevard - McMillan Park (Haskell Circle), Cameron Park (28 Avenue N). Other parks: Pinner Place Park (Pinner Place and Pridgen Road), Withers Park (2 Avenue S and Myrtle Street), Loblolly Park (Loblolly Circle, in the Dunes section), Memorial Park (Porcher Avenue and Haskell Circle), Springs Park (Springs Avenue and Hampton Circle).

CHAPIN PARK
(16th Avenue N and Kings Hwy) Located in the middle of downtown, the park has an arbor area, two-story gazebo, picnic tables, a wooden playground, and garden swings. The city allows festivals in the park, as well as other city functions and political events. Art shows and outdoor concerts are common on weekends.

FITNESS AND RENTALS

Visitors to Myrtle Beach do not have to leave their exercise routines behind. Or perhaps all the sand and relaxation is inspiring you to begin exercising. Along with the old standbys of recreation centers, tennis clubs, and gyms, there are shops that rent bikes or offer horseback riding. Sports enthusiasts will find plenty to do.

With so much accessible sand, it is no surprise that beach volleyball is popular in Myrtle Beach. The beach is packed with pickup games during the summer. Public nets are set up at Downwind Sails on 29 Avenue S, next to Damon's restaurant, and at Kingston Plantation, near Restaurant Row.

Biking is encouraged in Myrtle Beach, with clearly marked paths along the beach and Ocean Boulevard. The residential area north of 54 Avenue N features an outdoor fitness trail with exercise equipment. Many locations along the beach rent out bicycles and tricycles.

BIKE RENTALS
There are numerous locations around Myrtle Beach that will allow the bicycle enthusiast to enjoy a ride. **Bicycles N Gear** (515 US 501 ☎ 843.626.2453 ⌁ bikesngear.com) rents beach cruiser bikes and in-line skates on a daily rate. Rentals include

helmets and other protective gear. **501 Bike Shop** (1360 Highway 501 ☎ 843.445.6278) offers helmets, locks and baskets with every rental.

BEST VIEW FARM

(6129 Best Western Trail ☎ 843.650.7522) Since horses are not allowed on the beach during the busy summer season, very few stables in the area offer horseback riding. However, Best View Farm (originally known as Garling Farm) boards horses and offers riding lessons on 45 acres of densely wooded land.

GRAND STRAND YMCA

(904 65 St N ☎ 843.449.9622 ⌁.gsfymca.org) The local YMCA sponsor community events as well as offering kid-friendly activities such as T-ball, baseball, soccer, swim classes, and camps. Adult activities include co-ed volleyball, shag and ballroom dancing, and softball. Along with a free-weights center and exercise equipment, the center also has cardiovascular equipment and aerobics classes.

PEPPER GEDDINGS RECREATION CENTER

(3205 Oak St ☎ 843.918.2280) This recreation center has various programs, such as swimming lessons offered by the American Red Cross, water-exercise, lifeguard-certification, and water-safety. Professional trainers supervise the weight-training room. The facility has a 25-yard heated indoor swimming pool, softball, baseball and football fields, and lighted tennis courts.

Other than sports, the center also offers arts and crafts, dance classes, and card games. The center also coordinates city-sponsored aerobics, swimming and sport events.

GRANDE DUNES TENNIS CLUB
(US 17 Bypass ☎ 843.449.4486) The tennis club has ten composition courts, two of which are lighted. Court time is purchased in hourly increments. Along with a free backboard area, players can practice with the ball machine. Full-time instructors offer tennis lessons year-round. The club also offers a match setup service for players looking for players and a racquet stringing service along with its pro shop.

MYRTLE BEACH PUBLIC COURTS
(2 locations: 3200 Oak Street, US 17 and 20 Avenue S ☎ 843.918.2280) The two outdoor asphalt-surfaced courts on Oat Street are next door to the Myrtle Beach Recreation Center. The courts are lit for night play, but the recreation center and bathroom facilities are closed at night. The 20th Avenue South location has six asphalt-covered courts, restrooms, and outdoor water fountains. The courts also have lights for night play.

FITNESS ONE-ON-ONE
(Galleria Shopping Center, 9600 North Kings Hwy ☎ 843.449.6486) A one-on-one personalized-training facility, all exercise programs are individually tailored to your current fitness level and potential. The package includes a personal workout plan, nutrition advice, cardiovascular exercise, and weight training. Programs for weight-loss, body toning, body-building, and spot training are offered. The club also has tanning facilities.

SPECTATOR SPORTS

If you are more of a watcher, than a do-er, Myrtle Beach offers a few ways to get your vicarious game on.

MYRTLE BEACH SPEEDWAY

(4300 US 501 ☎ 843.236.0500 ⌐.myrtlebeachspeedway.com) Amateur and professional drivers race on this track. Races are usually held Saturday nights, and feature five divisions: ministock, late-model stock, street stock, chargers, and trucks. The local season includes the Winston Racing Series, All-Pro, NASCAR Dash, Open Wheel Modified, and Busch Grand National series.

Concession items include beer, soft drinks, and snack foods, such as hot dogs, chips, and candy. You are also allowed to bring small hand-held coolers. Blankets or cushions are recommended for the stadium-style seats. Admission rates vary by the race.

MYRTLE BEACH PELICANS

(1251 21 Ave N ☎ 843.918.6000 ⌐ myrtlebeachpelicans.com) A Class-A affiliate for the Atlanta Braves, the Pelicans are part of the Carolina League. The $12 million **Coastal Federal Field** has 2,676 box seats and 1,481 reserved seats that were brought over from the old Fulton County Stadium, the original home of the Braves. The field is visible from lounges, suites, patio boxes, and picnic areas. There is also a wheelchair-accessible children's playground on premises.

Parking is free at the field. Specials, such as dollar drafts, are common. The "Steel in Time" steel-drum band and Dinger the Home Run Dog (a yellow retriever) entertain the crowds.

Myrtle Beach has over 13 million visitors each year, but the city itself has a full-time population of around 25,000.

Entertainment

Music variety shows are a Myrtle Beach standard, combining rock, country, and bluegrass music with a dose of comedy, Christianity, and patriotism. There are also plenty of bars and clubs, with live music or DJs spinning the tunes.

SHOWS

Shows and entertainment venues were scarce in Myrtle Beach before 1986. People believed that there were not enough people in the area to support the entertainment industry on a year-round basis. Then Calvin Gilmore opened the Carolina Opry and proved there were enough visitors coming year-round to buy the tickets. Shows were sold out in advance; tickets to the Christmas show were sold out by June.

SHOW TIPS AND TICKETS
The live performances at Myrtle Beach range from musicals, concerts, and variety shows. Some are family-oriented; others are not. Tickets are sold ahead of time, and are subject to change, so call and confirm ticket prices before purchasing. Refreshments are sold at most venues before each show, and during intermission. Some places serve alcohol.

For holiday shows, it's best to book the tickets at least six months in advance. It's not uncommon for the theaters to start compiling their waiting lists for the holiday shows by June.

Various discounts are available at the Tourist Office at Broadway at the Beach. It is worth it to stop by the tourist office to inquire about discounts for specific shows. The staff there can also make reservations for you.

CAROLINA OPRY

(Mile marker 204, North Kings Highway, at US 17 Bypass, 8901 Highway 17 North ☎ 843.913.4000 🖱 thecarolinaopry.com) The Carolina Opry offers something for everyone in its two-hour variety show. A little bit of country music, a little bit of jazz and a little mix of Nashville, Broadway, and Las Vegas. The performance showcases singers, musicians, comedians, and dancers.

Regardless of where you sit in the 2,200-seat hall, three giant screens and a premier sound and lighting system ensure every seat has a great view of what is happening.

The 30-member cast also performs a "Good Vibrations" show – a 90-minute virtual tour of the popular music of the baby boomer generation. As part of the tour, the cast zips through 60s, 70s, and 80s, such as the Righteous Brothers, Kiss, Elvis, and Beatles. This show has no intermission.

The Carolina Opry Christmas Special continues to pack the house every year. Performances for the holiday show begin in the first week of November and continue till the New Year. There are two shows on weekends, at 1pm and 7pm. During the week, there is only one performance, beginning at 7pm. There is a 15-minute pre-show prior to the beginning of the main performance.

Tickets can be purchased through a variety of trip-planning companies as well as the Opry web site. Shows tend to begin at 8pm, except for November and December (Holiday Show has different schedules). Ticket prices vary by age, with categories for adults, children, seniors, and students. Reservations are recommended and call ahead to verify ticket prices.

DIXIE STAMPEDE [MUST SEE]

(North Kings Hwy at US 17 Bypass, 8901-B Highway 17 North ☎ 843.497.9700 🖱 dixiestampede.com) Owned and developed by the Dollywood Theme Park Association, the Stampede is part dinner

attraction, part rodeo-style show. Dolly Parton had a hand in developing this $5 million dinner attraction. Tickets cover a show, dinner, and pre-show entertainment.

Before the main show begins, guests can relax in the Carriage Room and listen to live musical entertainment. Popcorn and peanuts are available, as well as soda and specialty fruit drinks (non-alcoholic) served in a collector series Souvenir Boot Mug. The Carriage Room Show begins approximately 50 minutes before the main show.

The horses are on display from 10 AM until show time on the horse walk outside the arena. It is free to see the horses there.

The menu features country cooking, including creamy vegetable soup, whole rotisserie chicken, hickory smoked barbecue pork loin, corn on the cob, herb-basted potato, homemade biscuit, and flaky apple pastry. Vegetarian meals are available upon request – the request must be made when making reservations. Unlimited drinks – Pepsi, tea, or coffee - are served. Singing waiters and waitresses provide warm wet towels for you to wipe your hands on after your meal.

The show's themes evoke the romance of the "Old South" and the rivalry of the Civil War. Audience participation is encouraged. There are plenty of Southern belles, glitzy costumes that light up in the dark, trick-riding cowboys, and over thirty horses. The grand finale has over 15,000 sparkling lights, fireworks, and flying doves.

As part of the "North vs. South" theme, the show has an ostrich race. A jockey in Union blue and another in Confederate grey race each other on seven-foot tall birds around the arena. There's even a pig race between Ulysses S. Grant and Robert E. Lee. A pageant of horses and riders in red, white, and blue come together to perform "Color Me America" – as written and recorded by Dolly Parton.

The audience sits stadium-style around the arena, which seats approximately 1,000. Reservations are highly recommended; the place is regularly packed. Children 3 and under do not need tickets if they sit on an adult's lap and share the meal. Children between 4 and 11 are half-price. Ticket prices may change mid-season, so always call for current prices.

Shows tend to begin at 6 PM from March through May and September through October everyday. There are two shows, at 6 PM and at 8 PM, everyday from June through August. There are shows only on Monday, Wednesday, Friday, and Saturday, in November and December, starting at 6 PM.

Starting from mid-November until New Year's Eve, the Stampede performs the "Christmas at Dixie" show. Instead of the North/South rivalry, the show adopts a North Pole vs. South Pole rivalry. As part of the holiday show, elves serve the feast and Santa arrives in his sleigh. The trick rider wears the tin soldier costume, and belles discuss who celebrates Christmas more stylishly, the North or the South. There's a live Nativity scene, complete with the three wise men on camels.

Tickets are a bit more expensive than the usual show, and the cut-off-age for children is 17, not 11. Ticket prices do not reflect tax or gratuity. There are discounts for groups of 20 or larger. The arena is also wheelchair accessible.

Video cameras, photography, and other recording devices are not allowed in the arena.

COMEDY CABANA

(9588 North Kings Hwy ☎ 843.449.4242 ↻ comedycabana.com)
Calling itself a "5-star" comedy club (whatever that means), the cabana features three new professional comedians each week. The club has two rooms – a bar & grill and the theater room. The bar & grill is open before and after shows, serving food and

drink including appetizers, pizza, steak, sandwiches, chicken, and pasta. Dinner is also served during the show.

The theater room has intimate seating, and each person is required to buy at least two drinks during the course of the evening. The bar is fully stocked and there is also a selection of non-alcoholic drinks, including coffee, sparking water, and soft drinks.

Doors open early; around 6:30. Performances are on average two hours long and begin at about 8 PM in the spring and fall. The club is closed Sundays and Mondays. There is only one show – 8 PM – on Tuesdays to Thursdays. Fridays and Saturdays have an additional show that starts at 10:15. Comedy Cabana, however, is open everyday during the summer.

There is usually a cover charge (as well as the two-drink minimum). Reservations are highly recommended.

MEDIEVAL TIMES DINNER AND TOURNAMENT

(2904 Fantasy Way ☎ *888.935.6878* ꜛ *medievaltimes.com)*
Medieval Times has become a kind of staple to the modern tourist town, with numerous locations across the country. These unique four-course dinner shows features Andalusian stallions, the joust, sword fights, and loud (but predominately family-friendly) fun.

The fun begins as you cross a drawbridge to enter the 11th Century Spanish castle. The Count and Countess of Perelada, the lord and lady of the castle, greet you as you enter and personally invite you to join the banquet feast and to watch the knights in the tournament. Trumpeters herald the guests into the Grand Ceremonial Arena, where the banquet is served.

The four-course meal - the "bill of fare" - consists of garlic bread, vegetable soup, roasted chicken, spare ribs, and herb-basted potatoes. Pastry of the castle makes up dessert. Expect to eat without any utensils.

As part of the tournament audience, you will see falconry, sorcery, jousting matches, sword fights, and other tournament games such as ring pierce, flag toss, and the javelin throw. Horses perform intricate drills.

Six knights compete to become the Champion of the Evening. At the end of the competition, he champion chooses his Queen of Love and Beauty from the audience and crowns her as his queen.

Children under the age of three are admitted for free, and children under the age of 12 are half-price. The tickets cover show, dinner, and two rounds of drinks (alcohol or non-alcohol). Prices do not include tax or gratuity. Reservations are recommended.

The castle is fully enclosed, air conditioned, and wheelchair accessible.

HOUSE OF BLUES

(4640 Highway 17 S ☎ 843.272.3000 ⌁ hob.com) The House of Blues is a theme restaurant and entertainment venue in North Myrtle Beach. Visible from US 17, it looks decidedly shabby, an image intentionally cultivated. The 43,000 square foot structure was built with used architectural and construction material. The 700-seat capacity restaurant also has an outdoor deck ("Sugar Shack") and an 1800-seat capacity concert hall. The House of Blues is also covered with more than 5,000 original paintings and sculptures by more than 60 artists from around the country. The deep porches and covered walkways double as an open-air gallery. There are places to sit and relax in the Charleston-influenced courtyard. Even if you aren't planning to eat, you can just walk through the gates for a look around.

House of Blues is famous for its Sunday gospel brunch. Every Sunday morning, gospel groups perform in the concert hall, and the restaurant provides a banquet of grits, biscuits, roast beef, shrimp and rice, sausage, and bread pudding. The "kicks" entertainment section of Friday's Sun News usually lists the acts scheduled for that Sunday brunch.

FINE AND PERFORMING ARTS

The arts and cultural organizations in the area tend to cluster their events during the tourist off-season, from September to April. Arts councils such as The Waccamaw Arts and Crafts Guild (☎ 843.238.4628) for visual arts have monthly meetings with demonstrations, slide presentations, panel discussions, and shows exhibiting member works. The guild also sponsors a fall and spring show every year.

THE LONG BAY SYMPHONY
(Long Bay Youth Orchestra, 1551 21 Avenue N, ☎ 843.448.8379 ⟨⁜ longbaysymphony.com) The Long Bay Symphony performs classical, chamber, and pops music in approximately 12 concerts every season. The symphony also plays the original score during a showing of a silent film. Call or refer to the web site for concert information and ticket prices.

The symphony also promotes its 60-member youth orchestra. The orchestra performs two or three times a year, and once with the full symphony.

GRAND STRAND SENIORS FOR THE PERFORMING ARTS
(1268 21 Avenue N ☎ 843.626.3991) This group of performers aged 50 and over produces at least three shows a year. In the past, the group has put on *Send Me No Flowers, Arsenic and Old Lace,* and *Fiddler on the Roof.* Call for a current schedule.

CONCERTS

The Trinity Episcopal Church (3000 N Kings Hwy, ☎ 843.448.8426 ⌁ trinityepiscopalchurch.net) and the **First Presbyterian Church** (1300 N Kings Hwy ☎ 843.448.4496 ⌁ myrtlebeachpresbyterianchurch.org) offer concert series. Trinity typically has five primary concerts, a pipe organ series, and a kid matinee. In the past, the Vienna Choir Boys performed in the series. Past concerts have featured Gilbert and Sullivan productions and Handel's Messiah. The First Presbyterian concert series offer a variety of performances, including classical, pop, and Broadway selections. Every year, the church's Best of Broadway performance is sold out.

The Coastal Concert Association (☎ 843.449.7546) organizes concerts featuring brass ensembles, Big Band, Broadway musicals, symphonies, and dance groups. Performances are held at **Myrtle Beach High School Music and Arts Center** (3300 Central Pkwy; ☎ 843.448.7149). Tickets are usually available at the door, and discounted tickets are available for full-time students and everyone under 21 years of age. Call for current show schedules. **Carolina Master Chorale** (☎ 843.444.5774 ⌁ carolinamasterchorale.org) offers four concert performances throughout the year. Tickets for their concerts are available both in advance and at the door. Student tickets are available with valid ID.

NIGHTLIFE

Make sure you have your photo ID! While some places will let you in if you are underage (below 21), you will need photo ID to buy alcohol. Drinking and driving is strictly punished, so don't try. And don't buy alcohol for the minors (and there are *plenty* of minors).

South Carolina still serves alcohol in mini-bottles, as opposed to the rest of the country. The mini-bottles contain nearly two ounces of liquor as opposed to the normal one ounce. Mixed drinks tend to cost more since bars charge for each mini-bottle opened to make the drink.

Local laws restrict alcohol sales after 2 AM on Saturday and Sunday. If you have a drink in front of you after 2 AM on the weekend, you can be fined $200. For this reason, most places close by 2 AM on the weekend, saving Friday for the late nights (if any), to close at 4.

Dancing

Especially in the summer, there always seems to be a party at Myrtle Beach. And where there's a party, there's dancing. Following are a few of the more popular places to get your groove on.

2001 VIP ENTERTAINMENT
(920 Lake Arrowhead Rd ☎ 843.449.9434 ↺ 2001nightclub.com)
One of the longest running nightlife complexes in the community, 2001 has two separate nightclubs and a private lounge. There is a place to dance, and a place to relax. DJs play Top-40 music at the Echelon Dance Club. The Razzies Beach Club next door play the softer Top-40 music, beach music and oldies. The club also has a resident "Show Band" which performs every night. Carribays Island Bar is the lounge perfect to relax and listen to guest musicians play. Bars are all over 2001, and valet parking is available. While casual dress is allowed, hats and tank tops are not. The club is open year-round well past midnight. In the winter, the club may limit its nights. Admission fee depends on various factors: special nights, featured entertainment, and season.

BEACH WAGON

(906 South Kings Hwy ☎ 843.448.5918 ✆ beachwagonnitelife.com)
The Beach Wagon features live concerts and all-night two-step in a long dance halls. Country music stars like Marty Stuart, John Anderson, Sweethearts of the Rodeo, Aaron Tippin, and McBride & The Ride played here before making it big. Free dance lessons are available during some nights. The club offers ladies' nights, when they are allowed in free. The club's house band, "Silver" plays several nights a week. Open every night during the season, the club is open on limited nights in the winter. Call ahead for hours.

DEAD DOG SALOON

(760 Coastal Grand Circle ☎ 843.839.3647 ✆ deaddogsaloon.com)
Live bands play at the Dead Dog several nights a week. The eatery is famous in the area, and there's no cover charge. The place has a great patio for parties, and on Saturdays the saloon hosts cookouts. The band moves out on to the patio on warm days.

The original location is in Murrells Inlet. This second location a massive two-story log cabin located near Coastal Grand Mall. Along with an outdoor patio, the cabin has three bandstands, two bars, and total restaurant seating for over 300 patrons.

MOTHER FLETCHER'S

(Eight Avenue N & Ocean Blvd ☎ 843.448.2545) Mother Fletcher's holds several contests for its female patrons – ranging from wet T-shirt contest, skirt flirt contest, and the legs contest. Ladies Night is also popular. The club has a double oceanfront deck and plays dance tunes all night, every night during the summer.

STUDEBAKER'S
(2000 North Kings Hwy ☎ 843.448.9747 studebakersclub.com) The dance club plays everything from Motown to old school to retro. Open every night in the summer, the hours are abbreviated in the off-season; call ahead for hours and cover charges.

BUMMZ ON THE BEACH
(2002 North Ocean Blvd ☎ 843.916.9111) A beachfront garden café, Bummz on the Beach has a pine interior and a large beach patio. Swimsuits are just fine for partying at Bummz. The place offers live music entertainment every night. The type of entertainment varies with the season. Call ahead to find out when karaoke nights are.

WARREN'S RESTAURANT & LOUNGE
(1108 Third Avenue S ☎ 843.448.3110) Warren's has karaoke every night from 8:30 PM to 2 AM. A lot of the singers are serious talents and the place is usually full. A full dinner menu featuring steaks and prime rib is available on weekends.

SPORTS BARS

These sports bars have at least four TVs showing sporting events, and showing at least two games at a time. There may or may not be a cover charge, depending on the sporting event(s) being promoted at the time. In most cases, the bars open in the afternoon and close very late; but hours vary depending on the season, so call ahead for specific information.

DROOPY'S
(5201 North King's Hwy ☎ 843.449.2620) Droopy's has more than 14 televisions, 2 pool tables, lots of video games, and a Foosball table. Basic appetizers and sandwiches are served, along

with some daily specials. During football season, the bar opens earlier on days the NFL schedules early games.

FOSTER'S CAFÉ & BAR
(6307-A North Kings Hwy ☎ 843.449.7945) Foster's has more than half a dozen televisions, darts, and a pool table. While small, it's a popular place for the locals. It has decent bar comfort food and a somewhat crowded, claustrophobic atmosphere.

JIMMAGAN'S PUB SPORTS BAR
(6003 North Kings Hwy ☎ 843.497.5450) Jimmagan's has 35 TVs, pool tables, and electronic darts. A favorite bar amongst the biker crowd, the menu is limited to sandwiches, burgers, and some finger foods. The wings are cheap. The bar guarantees that you can see every Sunday NFL game during football season.

MARVIN'S
(918 North Ocean Blvd ☎ 843.448.4926) This oceanfront bar has over 80 feet of windows overlooking the Atlantic Ocean. Along with pool tables, Marvin's also has a collection of NASCAR memorabilia. The food served here is basic: chicken wings, pizza, nachos, burgers, dogs, sandwiches, fried foods, and appetizers.

MURPHY'S LAW SPORTS BAR
(405 South Kings Hwy ☎ 843.448.6021) Murphy's Law has electronic darts, golf game, and 25 television sets. Two pool tables are set up in the middle of the chairs and tables in this bar.

The sandwiches at Murphy's Law are huge: there's a "50-yard" steak sandwich as well as "100-yard" sandwich. It's recommended for two people to share the 100-yarder. Chicken wings are popular. The menu also offers a raw bar, including oysters, clams, steamed shrimp, and crab legs. The bar also sells draft beer during happy hours.

SHAMROCK'S SPORTS BAR & GRILL

(2510 North Kings Hwy ☎ 843.448.2532) Shamrock's has 20 beers on tap and offers them in 20-ounce pints. A pitcher is very reasonably priced. The Munchie Special appeases late-night hunger pangs, by offering everything on the Munchie Menu at half-price between 9 PM to 1 AM during the week. The Buffalo wings, skins, nachos, and other fried foods are popular. The menu also includes soups, salads, sandwiches, and other specialty plates.

Where to Eat

There is no shortage of places to eat in Myrtle Beach, and no single book can list every eatery. While most places are mid-range, competition keeps prices reasonable.

Price Guide:
$	=	< $20
$$	=	$21 to $35
$$$	=	$36 to $50
$$$$	=	> $50

Most area lodgings have an in-house restaurant and bars often have a kitchen offering a full menu. The stretch of Highway 17 between Myrtle Beach and North Myrtle Beach is called **Restaurant Row** because of its heavy concentration of eateries. There are also many places to eat at the Broadway at the Beach entertainment complex (see the *Broadway at the Beach* chapter for those restaurants).

Even though the city is right on the ocean, Myrtle Beach, for the most part, is a ham and potatoes town. Seafood, ironically, is not a specialty. Locals go to other parts of the Grand Strand, namely the nearby fishing village of Murrells Inlet, also known as the state's seafood capital.

Calabash, a fishing village 25 miles north of Myrtle Beach, is by the state border with North Carolina. Calabash is famous for its fresh seafood meals, and many local Myrtle Beach restaurants have incorporated the name into the menu. Locally, Calabash seafood refers to deep-fried seafood served hot.

There are plenty of national chains including Friendly's, Cracker Barrel, Shoney's, Red Lobster, Olive Garden, and T.G.I. Friday's. Fast food places also exist. For American ambience, hit the burger bars on Ocean Blvd near the amusement parks. International cuisine, like Thai, Japanese, and Mediterranean, are harder to find, but available. As more people from other parts of the country settle down to make Myrtle Beach their home year-round, the local cuisine has expanded.

Most places are casual dress, allowing shorts and t-shirts, although bathing suits and flip-flops will be frowned upon in most places. The most laid-back beachfront places will allow them, though. And if you are in the mood for a dressy evening, with a suit or long gown, that's here, too.

Many restaurants do not accept reservations. As a result, long lines are very common, especially at the more casual places during the peak season. It's recommended to call just before going to find out what the wait time is. The drop-by-and-see approach works, too, since there are always other dining options. Most restaurants accept credit cards – at least Visa and MasterCard – for payment.

Most restaurants in Myrtle Beach use the alternate name for Highway 17 – Kings Highway – in their addresses.

The following table describes the key used to categorize each restaurant by price range. The calculation is performed on dinner for two for an "average" meal, without cocktails, tax, or tip. That means no specials or elaborate appetizers. Lunch is usually half (or a third) of what dinner costs.

SEAFOOD

Despite its oceanfront location and plethora of available seafood, Myrtle Beach is not a "seafood" place. While the restaurants are mostly competent in their preparations of seafood, only a few stand out as really exceptional

DIRTY DON'S OYSTER BAR & GRILL
(408 21 Avenue N ☎ 843.448.4881) The menu at Dirty Don's features catfish fingers, oyster shooters, clams on the half shell, sandwiches, and seafood chowder. The steaks are juicy and the shrimps are king-sized. ($$)

FLAMINGO SEAFOOD GRILL
(7100 North Kings Hwy ☎ 843.449.5388 flamingogrill.com) The décor is art-deco: black lacquer with pink and blue neon accents. Owned by the same people who own Cagney's Old Place, the menu includes lots of fresh seafood. Pasta, chicken, prime rib, and steak are also offered. There's also a separate children's menu. Flamingo is open only for dinner, everyday. ($$$)

SEA CAPTAIN'S HOUSE [MUST SEE]
(3002 North Ocean Blvd ☎ 843.448.8082 seacaptains.com) The building was originally a beach cottage, and from the outside, it still looks like one. The dining experience features delicious food and panoramic views of the Atlantic Ocean. The cuisine is both seafood and Southern. The restaurant is open for breakfast, lunch, and dinner. ($$$)

STEAKHOUSES

Good steaks, fine wine, fresh seafood (of course), and a classy ambience make up many of the Myrtle Beach area's better steakhouses.

NEW YORK PRIME
(405 28 Avenue N ☎ 843.448.8081 newyorkprime.com) The owners opened New York Prime after eating at some of New York City's best steakhouses: Peter Luger's, The Palm, and Smith and Wollensky. The owners aim to offer the New York-style steakhouse experience in Myrtle Beach. To achieve that goal, they've picked slaughterhouses that meet their specifications and buy quality cuts. The rest of the food is also top-quality: the freshest fish, giant live lobsters, and freshest vegetables. The wine cellar is also extensive.

Since the meat is of exemplary quality, spices and tenderizers are unnecessary in cooking. Cuts are extra thick and cooked in ceramic broilers that reach a temperature of over a thousand degrees. ($$$$)

T-BONZ GILL & GRILL
(US 17 Bypass and 21 Avenue N ☎ 843.946.7111 🖰 tbonz.com) Located opposite the NASCAR Speedpark and Broadway at the Beach, the restaurant offers a fun dining experience. The interior is spacious and noisy. The dress is casual and kids are welcomed.

All portions are hearty, from beef, grilled chicken, vegetarian, and seafood. The specialty, shrimp-and-grits, is an example of Southern cooking. The bar features T-Bonz Homegrown Ales on tap.

Kids menu and take-out is available. For lunch the restaurant serves light fare. For late nights, the place becomes an after-hours social scene. There's a location in North Myrtle Beach, off US 17, as well. ($$)

THORNY'S STEAKHOUSE & SALOON
(600 S. Kings Hwy ☎ 843.448.2333) A basic steakhouse, Thorny's serves Danish Baby Back Ribs, several kinds of steak, and home style dinners. There's also an early bird special from 11 AM to 5:30 PM that includes steak tips, shrimp, and chicken, served with salad, potatoes, and yeast rolls. There is a children's menu called "Little Thorny Meals" for children under the age of ten. The kid meal includes fries, drink, and ice cream, and is served on a Frisbee.

INTERNATIONAL

This section includes a few Myrtle Beach restaurants that feature cuisine with a more international flair.

FIESTA DEL BURRO LOCO
(960 Jason Blvd, US 17 Bypass and 10 Avenue N ☎ 843.626.1756) The exterior of the building is intentionally weathered to look like old and straight out of Mexico. The interior has several murals, including the 45-foot-tall mural of a bullfight right at the entrance, a billboard collage covering the ceiling, and an upside-down Elvis presiding over the bar.

The food is Mexican, with the house specialty being the fajitas and the stuffed jalapenos. The staff hand squeeze the limes used in the margaritas, too. Open everyday for dinner, the restaurant does not require reservations. ($$)

VILLA MARE
(7819 North Kings Hwy ☎ 843.449.8654) This simple, unassuming Italian restaurant is located inside a strip mall. Dress is casual. The menu features standard Italian fare at affordable prices, including calzones and pastas. All dishes are made to order: veal, chicken parmigiana, shrimp piccata, fettuccine Alfredo and other pasta dishes.

Because the place is small and seating is limited, reservations are a must. The restaurant is closed on Sundays, and is open for dinner from Monday to Saturday. ($$)

ELEGANT DINING

For romantic or more formal affairs, following is a selection of Myrtle Beach's more upscale dining establishments. Please call ahead; some of these places are open for dinner only.

THE LIBRARY
(1212 North Kings Hwy ☎ 843.448.4527 ⌂ thelibraryrestaurantsc.com) An elegant restaurant, The Library offers European

cuisine. The décor resembles the inside of a library – hence the name. The walls are lined with bookcases holding works of literature.

Established in 1974, the Library Restaurant features wait staff in tuxedoes. The menu includes veal, seafood, duck, beef, and chicken. The Library is open only for dinner. ($$$$)

SEA ISLAND, AN INN ON THE BEACH
(6000 North Ocean Blvd ☎ 843.449.6406 ⌁ seaislandonthebeach.com) The inn's dining room caters mainly to the inn's guests, but outside guests are also allowed in limited numbers. All meals come with a beautiful ocean view. Breakfast is continental cuisine, as is dinner. However, dressy attire is required for dinner – men must wear coats. The chef at this full-service restaurant prepares a five-course meal every night; you choose between the five entrees. Along with seafood, there are chicken, beef, and veal choices. Because the restaurant is limited to the general public, reservations are required. ($$$$)

COLLECTORS CAFÉ AND GALLERY
(7726 North Kings Hwy ☎ 843.449.9370 ⌁ collectorscafeandgallery.com) Collectors Café and Gallery has something for everyone. In the mood for some elegant dining? No problem. Looking for something comfortable and casual? That's possible, too. Want to just lounge and relax, as if you are in your favorite coffeehouse back home? That's a snap. The restaurant manages this by having three different rooms with different ambiance and décor catering to different kinds of diners.

The café's elegant dining room has columns and high ceilings. Original paintings, seascapes and cityscapes, hang on the walls. Beyond the dining room, there is a grill room with and hand-tiled, bar-height tables. You can watch the chefs cook while seated at these tables. Oversized canvases also cover the walls with original art. Most of the art on display in the three rooms are available for purchase.

There's also a coffeehouse room that's even more relaxed. More original art – not just hanging canvases, but artwork – cover every surface, table, wall, and chair.

The cuisine here is Mediterranean, featuring foods like filet of beef carpaccio, pan-sautéed crab cakes and asparagus, roasted garlic turnip puree, pasta and salad selections, veal, and fresh seafood. Dessert is excellent – especially the tiramisu.

The gallery opens at noon from Monday to Saturday. The restaurant is open only for dinner, and reservations are highly recommended. ($$$$)

ROSSI'S

(The Galleria; 9639 US 17 N ☎ 843.449.0481) Rossi's serves veal, pasta, fresh seafood, and Black Angus beef, all in generous portions. Fine wines and a cozy dining room complete the experience. The dining room has weathered brick walls, stained glass, chandeliers, a piano bar, and live entertainment. ($$$)

SAM SNEAD'S TAVERN [MUST SEE]

(9708 North Kings Hwy ☎ 843.497.0580 samsneadstavern.com) Located in Restaurant Row, this tavern manages to seem cozy with its soft lights and polished wood surfaces. The walls are covered with golf memorabilia from Sam Snead's PGA career. A lot of the food is prepared in the wood-burning oven – you can smell burning oak when you walk in. The restaurant serves deep-fried wontons, chicken and peppers wrapped in a pastry. The ribs are hand-rubbed, oak-smoked, and served with homemade barbecue sauce. ($$)

CAGNEY'S OLD PLACE
(9911 North Kings Hwy, US 17 N and 71 Ave ☎ *843.449.0288* 🕏 *cagneysoldplace.com)* Cagney's offers both dinner and dancing. The house specialty here is the prime rib. A children's menu is also available. A little off the beaten track, this is place for surf and turf.

Most of the antiques up for show as part of the place's décor came from the old Ocean Forest Hotel. The hotel was demolished in 1974. ($$$)

CHESTNUT HILL
(9922 US 17 ☎ *843.449.3984* 🕏 *chestnuthilldining.com)* Situated smack in the middle of Restaurant Row, the restaurant sits next to a lake, under a grove of oak trees. The cheesecakes here are excellent. The majority of the seafood served here was caught on the restaurant's own boat earlier in the day. Now, that's fresh! ($$$)

CASUAL DINING

The section describes a few places to relax and enjoy a meal, without all the fanfare of a more upscale establishment.

AKEL'S HOUSE OF PANCAKES
(6409 North Kings Hwy ☎ *843.449.4815)* A local landmark, Akel's is popular for its service, pancakes, and atmosphere. The staff is friendly, and there is a sense of familiarity between diners. While it bills itself as a pancake house, the menu also lists sandwiches, salads and burgers.

Akel's is open all night, from 10 PM to 2PM. After a night on the town, this is a good place to get something to eat before going home and passing out. It's also a great place to go for a hearty breakfast before starting the day. ($)

CAROLINA ROADHOUSE 🚩

(4617 North Kings Hwy ☎ 843.497.9911) Carolina Roadhouse is part of a chain nationwide that includes California Dreaming, Frank Manzetti's and Joey D's. The restaurant has beautiful architecture, with soaring ceilings and arched windows. The beautiful interior design displays mirrors, lights are recessed to set the mood, and there is a spicy scent of cedar.

The service is outstanding, as well as the food. Barbecue chicken is tender and the ribs are melting-in-your-mouth-soft. The menu also includes steaks, seafood, salad (hot bacon and honey-mustard dressing on top), gumbo, and baked potato soup.

Open for lunch and dinner everyday, this restaurant actually takes reservations. Dress is casual here. ($$)

VINTAGE HOUSE CAFÉ

(1210 North Kings Hwy ☎ 843.626.3918) This café serves house dressings for its salads, such as raspberry vinaigrette and fresh herb. At least one soup is offered daily. The lunch menu features gourmet sandwiches, quiche, and other specials. The dinner menu is varied, and the dessert menu changes everyday. This is not the place to go if you are on a diet, unless you don't mind breaking it. Closed Sunday, the café serves lunch Monday to Saturday. Dinner, however, is served only from Tuesday to Saturday. ($$$)

DAGWOODS

(400 11 Avenue N ☎ 843.448.0100) The submarine sandwiches here are huge; multi-decker subs stuffed with everything. The prices are low for the amount of food you get, making it popular amongst vacationing college students. Fresh bread is baked daily, and the restaurant serves both hot and cold sandwiches. It is open everyday for lunch and dinner. ($)

RIVER CITY CAFÉ

(3 locations in Myrtle Beach: 404 21 Avenue N, ☎ 843.448.1990; 9550 Shore Drive, ☎ 843.497.5299; 208 73 Avenue N, ☎ 843.449.887 ✆ rivercitycafe.com) A wood-frame building resembling an old beach house, River City Café is a hamburger joint. The interior maintains the old beach house image, with worn wooden floors, benches, and chairs. The ceiling and walls are covered with car tags and bumper stickers.

Patrons help themselves to dry-roasted peanuts kept in a big bin and throw the shells to the floor. On busy nights, the floor is covered. Elegant dining experience this is not. The burgers, however, are huge, with a variety of fixings, such as thick slabs of cheese, jalapenos, lettuce, tomatoes, grilled onion, and bacon. The onion rings are also pretty big here. Other sandwiches and hot dogs are also served. ($)

The Myrtle Beach area has about 50 miniature golf courses — about half as many as there are full-size courses.

Where to Shop

Many of the stores along Ocean Boulevard and near the beach specialize in souvenirs and beachwear. At many of these shops, you can haggle to get the best bargain. With so many shops selling swimsuits, suntan products, sunshades, beach chairs, rafts, umbrellas, souvenir items, beach toys, T-shirts, and sportswear, it's easy to underestimate the shopping options Myrtle Beach has to offer.

Myrtle Beach is full of antique shops, booth rental flea markets where everything is a bargain, and plenty of name-brand retailers and outlets. The area also has mega golf and sporting goods stores, furniture and interior design stores, and art galleries. Some of the major retailers in the area are JCPenney, Saks, and Belk. There are three Wal-Marts in the area. The Waccamaw Regional Transportation Authority's bus routes stop at each Wal-Mart. There are plenty of small food-marts, as well as larger supermarket chains, including Kroger, Food Lion, and Winn-Dixie.

The Myrtle Beach Convention Center hosts shopping festivals and industry shows throughout the year. The annual Doll Show & Sale features lots of dolls, accessories, minor repairs, and doll-making supplies. Hundreds of crafts people display their work at the Craftsman Classic Arts & Crafts Festival. The Dickens Christmas Show & Festival displays and sells decorative items and gifts. Inspired by the *Christmas Carol*, the show takes place in an 18th century setting, complete with a Victorian Holiday Marketplace, strolling musicians, and tealeaf readers. Vendors in period dress hawk fine arts and crafts, décor, Christmas gifts, and toys. The festival also has Punch & Judy shows. Other festivals at the convention center are the Grand Strand Gift & Resort Merchandise Show and the Gun & Knife Show.

OUTLETS

Bargain-hunters love outlet malls, and the Myrtle Beach area is in no short supply of these hubs. Need I say more?

MYRTLE BEACH FACTORY STORES
(4635 Factory Stores Blvd ☎ 843.236.5100 ⌁ shopmyrtlebeach.com) Located on US Highway 501, the outlet center has nearly half a million square feet of stores clustered in a "village." With over 100 brand name stores, including Banana Republic, Perry Ellis, GAP, the factory stores claim to offer a savings up to 70 percent in retail prices.

TANGER OUTLETS
(10785 Kings Rd, Intersection of US 17 with Veterans Hwy ☎ 843.449.0491 ⌁ tangeroutlet.com) Located near Colonial Mall, the 43-acre complex cost nearly $50 million to build. The 40,0000 square foot retail space has over 50 outlet and specialty stores, including top brands such as Tommy Hilfiger, Nautica and Liz Claiborne. The Tanger Outlet is laid out in a pedestrian-friendly design and boasts landscaped courtyards and a food court.

WACCAMAW FACTORY SHOPPES
(3200 Pottery Dr ☎ 843.236.6152 ⌁ waccamawfactoryshoppes.com) Located where US 501 intersects with the Intracoastal Waterway, the outlets are only three miles away from downtown. Stores include Liz Claiborne and Dress Barn. The food court serves pizza, hamburgers, salads, and an assortment of international food. The complex offers free wheelchairs upon request.

Shopping Centers

While the suburban retail-shopping complex is an often-too-repeated experience best left out of a Tourist Town vacation, there are a few area gems.

MYRTLE SQUARE MALL
(17 Business at 26th Avenue N) The biggest mall in the area, the stores are arranged around a center court, dominated by a giant clock. Some of the stores include Belk, Body Shop, Champs Sports, FootLocker, General Nutrition Center, Kay-Bee Toys, Office Depot, Payless Shoesource, Radio Shack, Sears, Sunglass Hut, Waldenbooks, and Zales Jewelers. The mall also has movie theaters, food courts, and several restaurants attached.

COASTAL GRAND MALL
(2000 Coastal Grand Circle ☎ 843.839.9100) One of the area's newest malls has approximately 130 stores in all, with anchors such as Belk, Dillard's, Sears, Dick's Sporting Goods, and Bed Bath & Beyond. The mall also has movie theaters, food courts, and several restaurants attached.

COLONIAL MALL MYRTLE BEACH
(Hwy 17 North, at Highway 22 Conway Bypass ☎ 843.272.4040 ⌂ colonialmallmyrtlebeach.com) This new mall opened in 2006 and boasts a 12-screen stadium-seating theater, department stores, a children's' play area, specialty stores, and restaurants.

SPECIALTY STORES

When just any old gift won't do, Myrtle Beach has more than its share of specialty stores. Of course, there are many more at Myrtle Beach than are listed here.

CHRISTMAS ELEGANCE
(4301 North Kings Hwy ☎ 843.626.3100) Some people like to do their Christmas shopping in July. Here at Christmas Elegance, it's the season every single day of the year. Featuring seven stores in a natural setting, shoppers will find music boxes, collectors' dolls, electric trains, yard ornaments, handmade jewelry, candles, and cards. There's also a cutlery shop, and of course, a variety of holiday decorations everywhere. If you need a gift for an occasion other than Christmas, never fear. The stores carry non-Christmas merchandise as well.

GAY DOLPHIN
(916 North Ocean Blvd at Ninth Avenue N ☎ 843.448.6550 ⌂ gaydolphin.com) The Gay Dolphin's extensive inventory number more than 60,000 items. This gift shop sells a variety of things, including postcards and collectibles. The shop also houses several smaller shops inside, arranged in "coves" of similar merchandise. There are over 50 coves, featuring an assortment of products such as stuffed animals, souvenirs, golf memorabilia, shark's teeth, toys, swimwear, ceramics, and shells. The small stores in Collector's Cove sell Hummel figurines, clowns, gnomes, and bells.

RAINBOW HARBOR
(Kings Hwy at 49 Avenue N ☎ 843.449.7476) The stores on this strip specialize in fine furnishings and luxury items. The Gaye Sanders Fisher Gallery showcases local watercolors by the art-

ist/owner. Femme Fatal is a popular and high quality clothing and accessory store for women. The Melting Pot offers fondue. There are kitchen stores, jewelers, and shops selling interior furnishings.

LA PLAGE

(2304 N Kings Hwy at 23 Avenue N ☎ 843.626.2719 🖰 laplageswimwear.com) La Plage claims to be the largest swimwear specialty shop on the East Coast. While that claim may or may not be true, the shop does carry a wide selection of swimsuits (the store claims over 10,000) to fit all body types, including long torso, mastectomy, plus sizes, maternity, children's, and preteens. The store carries designer suits, such as Tara Grinna swimsuits and Kirsti Grinna's KGB bikini line. The store has surf wear, bikinis, cover ups, resort wear, custom swimwear and accessories.

Broadway at the Beach

(1325 Celebrity Circle at 21 Avenue N, ☎ 843.444.3200 🖰 broadwayatthebeach.com) Conceived by Burroughs & Chapin Company, Broadway at the Beach complex is an entertainment venue, a restaurant district, nightclub area, and a shopping village, all rolled into one massive overload of tourism pleasure. There are dozens of restaurants, several entertainment venues, a multi-screen **IMAX** theater, and a street packed with nightclubs. It is a 350-acre development, $250-million monster of an attraction. And it is all built around a man-made 23-acre Lake Broadway.

The complex opened in 1995 and quickly became the top tourist draw in South Carolina. And this is no surprise – there are some big names here, like **Ripley's Aquarium**. The area also offers some great nightlife. It is strictly tourist, but even many locals as well, desperate to get away from the beach scene, will make their way to this nearby paradise of bars, restaurants, eclectic stores, and unusual attractions. It is an outdoor themed shopping mall that rivals the behemoths of Orlando (and, to a lesser and more family-friendly extent, Las Vegas).

The **tourist office** in the complex offers a variety of discount coupons, show discounts, and lots of information about things to do. Even if you are not watching a show, it's worth swinging by the tourist office for the coupons to restaurants and other attractions.

Anyone can splash around in the lake on paddleboats. **Miss Broadway Water Taxi** offers rides on the lake. Food for the ducks and fish is sold in little dispensers on the boardwalk, if you want to feed the ducks. And for children, there are padded play spots, such as the Carousel Park.

THEMED AREAS

These days, something almost can't pass for a tourist attraction if it doesn't offer some kind of out-of-location themed environment. Don't worry; in this aspect Broadway at the Beach does not disappoint. The complex has over a hundred shops, which are divided into one of the three districts: **Caribbean Village**, **Charleston Boardwalk**, and **New England Village**. **Celebrity Square** consists of hot spots that feature musical acts. There are signed handprints in the cement on Celebrity Square from over thirty celebrities, such as Donna Summers, Johnny Mathis, Barry Manilow, and Wayne Newton.

ATTRACTIONS

Following are some of the more prominent attractions at Broadway at the Beach. As you'll note when paying this area a visit, however, there are indeed many things to see and do here.

RIPLEY'S AQUARIUM [MUST SEE]
(Broadway at the Beach, 1110 Celebrity Circle ☎ *843.916.0888* ⌁ *ripleysaquarium.com)* The $40 million state of the art aquarium houses some of the most beautiful (and dangerous) aquatic life. The 87,000 square foot aquarium has several exhibits and displays, highlighting different species.

The most elaborate, fascinating, and beautiful attraction at the aquarium is the Dangerous Reef – a 750,000-gallon tank. Visitors walk through the tank along a 330-foot moving glide path inside the tunnel. Sharks swim next to you, over you, separated only by the (thick!) glass. The experience is akin to walking on the ocean floor, since the glass tunnel meanders through the tank.

Rainbow Rock show thousands of brilliant Pacific fish swimming amongst a reef. Ray Bay, a multi-level display, with rocks and a sandy beach, highlights several species of rays. At Friendship Flats, visitors can touch Atlantic and Southern Cow-Nose Rays and Bonnet Head Sharks. The Rio Amazon exhibit showcases the Amazon rain forest with species including the piranha. The Living Gallery features Pacific giant octopus, sea anemones, living corals, jellies, weedy sea dragons, sea horses, and pipefish. There are dive shows and marine education classes.

The aquarium offers a "sleep with the sharks" program, where visitors can spend the night at the aquarium and have various interactive classes.

MAGIQUEST

(Broadway at the Beach, 1185 Celebrity Circle ☎ 843.913.9460 magiquestmb.com) Definitely for children, but teens might also enjoy it, MagiQuest is a hard thing to explain. When described on paper (like you're about to read) it sounds too much like a video game to be taken seriously. But when you pay the fee, equip your wand, and enter the MagiQuest arena, you really do what is described. Well, almost.

You "choose" a magic wand at the start of the adventure. You quest through 20,000 square foot game space to learn how to use the wand and increase your powers. The wand can enchant over 250 different "artifacts" and "effects." Gold gathered during the quest can be redeemed at the gift shop for prizes, or increased magic powers for the wand. There are many quests, including rescuing the unicorn, battling the goblin king, returning the jewels to the princess, and fighting the mighty red dragon.

Actually, this is a surprisingly pleasant diversion. If you enjoy waving your wand at various electronic sensors and computer screens in a kind of plastic, indoor medieval wonderland, while dodging children who are running around doing the exact same thing, then you'll probably get a kick out of this little inventive experience.

The game has twelve quests, one for each "rune of power" – and then five master magi adventures. Inside the gift shop, you can challenge others to a duel, where you will cast spells at each other using a display screen that can sense the wand motions. The wand is programmed with where you stopped in the game, and what you did, so you can leave and come back at will. In fact, the game demands re-visits – don't expect to accomplish everything on your first try.

CAROUSEL PARK
(Broadway at the Beach ☎ *843.918.8737* ⌁ *broadwayatthebeach.com)* The Carousel Park features a classic carousel, a balloon Ferris wheel, and several rides, such as the Red Baron airplanes, the Little Drummer Boy ride, and the Broadway Train. Season passes give you access to unlimited rides.

IMAX DISCOVERY THEATER
(Broadway at the Beach ☎ *843.444.3333)* The screen is six stories tall and the theater plays the sound over a six-track digital sound system. Food can be purchased at the IMAX Café and gifts and toys at the gift shop. IMAX tickets tend to be pricier than regular movie theaters.

THE PALACE THEATRE
(Broadway at the Beach, 1420 Celebrity Circle ☎ *843.448.9224* ⌁ *palacetheatermyrtlebeach.com)* Check the web site to find out what shows are playing, or call ahead of time for the schedule and tickets. The web site also has special offers for shows. Some performances at the Palace: Le Grande Cirque – with its acrobatics and gymnastics, the Dean Martin Variety Show with perform-

ances "by" superstars such as Marilyn Monroe, Liza Minnelli, and Cher.

The Palace Theatre is built in a 1950's style and its cupola dome is visible from miles around. The antebellum structure is luxurious on the inside, with a large foyer, winding staircase, enormous marble columns, and glittering chandeliers.

The theater seats 2,700 and has a state of the art lighting and sound system.

DRAGON'S LAIR FANTASY GOLF
(Broadway at the Beach, Hwy 17 ☎ 843.913.9301) The Dragon's Lair has two courses, one featuring a fire-breathing dragon and the other, rampaging Vikings. Situated across from MagiQuest, the volcanic mountain is accessible by a bridge spanning the lake from one side. The volcano belches smoke in regular intervals. Players putt around, inside, and through the mountain, as well as over water.

BUTTERFLY PAVILION
(Broadway at the Beach ☎ 843.839.4451) Featuring over two thousand native North American butterflies, the Butterfly Pavilion also includes a **Wild Encounters Theater**, a lorikeet aviary, a gift shop, and a restaurant.

The pavilion is a glass structure 40 feet high and encompasses over 9000 square feet of landscape reproducing the butterflies' natural habitats. Visitors can enter an English beehive and watch honeybees make honey, or crawl into a giant ant mound. The **Nature Zone Discovery Center** offers classes.

Fun Eating

Theme restaurants put on an elaborate show to attract customers looking for a fun, experience-filled, and bedazzling dining experience. The highest concentration of these restaurants in Myrtle Beach is, of course, right here at Broadway at the Beach.

JIMMY BUFFETT'S MARGARITAVILLE

(Broadway at the Beach, 1114 Celebrity Circle ☎ 843.448.5455 margaritavillemyrtlebeach.com) Located next to the lighthouse, Margaritaville is hard to miss. There's a Tiki Room, and the steamboat Euphoria docked outside. After dinner, the restaurant transitions into a swinging nightclub where dancing is a must and live bands perform every night of the week.

As the name indicates, margaritas are the drink of choice, although there are other boat drinks and the restaurant's very own Lone Palm Ale. The menu is "Floribbean" – featuring fresh seafood and standard American fare such as cheeseburgers ("in paradise", for Parrotheads). ($$)

HARD ROCK CAFÉ [MUST SEE]

(Broadway at the Beach) Hard Rock Café is arguably the most recognized and picturesque place at Broadway at the Beach. Along the US 17 Bypass, the restaurant is inside a huge pyramid covered with hieroglyphics. Palm trees surround the pyramid and the parking lot. At night, spotlights light up the pyramid. The only Hard Rock Café built in this shape, sphinxes guard the entrances. A lighted fountain is also in front of the main entrance.

The interior is stone, and covered with more hieroglyphics. Rock'n'roll displays and memorabilia cover all available walls. When you enter, you are actually a level above the dining room, giving you an excellent view of what everyone else is having.

The menu offers a variety of options to fit different diets, including vegetarian foods and Southern barbecue. ($$)

NASCAR CAFÉ
(Broadway at the Beach) South of the Hard Rock Café's distinctive pyramid, also on US 17 Bypass, are the checkered flags of NASCAR Café. The restaurant has a 20-acre racetrack on premises. A wax figure of Bill France, NASCAR's founder, stands at the beginning of the course. Many of the displays are devoted to racing legends. Thirteen racecars are suspended from the ceiling.

Upon entering the restaurant, patrons have to cross Bill France Boulevard, where people are looking at displays or playing video games. Inside the café, booths form a circular track around a massive bar.

The waitstaff are dressed in a sleek red jumpsuit and a headset. The dishes have NASCAR-themed names, such as Thunder Road Burgers, Longtrack Chili Dogs, and Chocolate Fudge Tire. ($$)

CADDYSHACK
(Broadway at the Beach) Caddyshack the restaurant is designed like a country club. The Murray Brothers - comedian Bill Murray and his five brothers, Brian, Joel, Joe, Andy, and Ed – encourage guests to "Eat Drink and Be Murray" at Caddyshack.

The 8,500-square-foot restaurant can easily accommodate 300 guests. The dining space opens onto a 3,000 square foot deck that overlooks the lake at Broadway at the Beach. The inside of the restaurant features the brothers, the sport of caddying (the Murrays all caddied as teenagers to earn tuition for Catholic school), and humor.

The Bunker Bar has several televisions, tuned to multiple sporting events. Looper's Lounge accommodates large groups and also doubles as a billiards room. The Shed is the gift shop, selling Murray Brothers merchandise such as t-shirts, hats, glasses, golf attire, and golf gadgets.

The menu is continental cuisine, such as wings, peel'n'eat shrimp, oversized salads, sandwiches, steaks, seafood, chicken, ribs, and pasta. ($$)

PLANET HOLLYWOOD MUST SEE!

(2915 Hollywood Dr. ☎ 843.448.7827 ✆ planethollywood.com) Planet Hollywood is across the street from Broadway at the Beach, on 25th Avenue. The building itself is literally shaped like a blue and green planet. The cement foundation is imprinted with various handprints and signatures from Hollywood stars.

Display cases are everywhere - between booths and around pillars. Faces of superstars, including Elvis Presley, George Clooney, Demi Moore, and others, form a two-story collage on the walls. The upholstery is animal print.

The food and drinks often take on the names of movies (*Cliffhanger*, *Terminator*, etc). The menu is a fusion of West Coast, Italian, and Asian. ($$)

BULLWINKLE'S FAMILY FOOD AND FUN

(Near Broadway at the Beach) The building evokes the Klondike with its split-log lodge. Inside, children can play in a towering soft play structure with slides, wobbling walkways, and a clubhouse. Parents are encouraged to go through the structure, as there are no age or size restrictions. The menu offers staple fare such as Rocky's Remarkable burgers and Klondike Fried Chicken. ($$)

LIBERTY STEAKHOUSE AND BREWERY

(Broadway at the Beach, 1321 Celebrity Circle ☎ 843.626.4677) A combination steakhouse and brewery, guests can enjoy beer brewed fresh every day and cut into a piece of succulent meat. On special drinking holidays, such as Oktoberfest and St. Pat-

rick's Day, the brewery prepares seasonal brews. There are six beers on tap everyday.

Everyone is invited to take the tour of the brewery and watch as brewers make the beers. At the end of the tour is a beer-making demonstration.

The food is hearty standard fare, except served in large portions. There are specialty cuts of beef, burgers, and appetizers such as buffalo shrimp. Brick-oven pizzas are also available. The restaurant is open for both lunch and dinner everyday. ($$)

TONY ROMA'S – A PLACE FOR RIBS

(Broadway at the Beach, 1317 Celebrity Circle ☎ *843.448.7427* 🖰 *tonyromas.com)* Several rib flavors are served here: original baby backs, Carolina Honeys (honey and molasses), Blue Ridge Smokies (hint of molasses laced with burning wood), Tony Roma's Red Hots (five types of peppers), and Bountiful Beef Ribs (big, juicy, and smoky). Along with ribs, there are salads, grilled specialties, a few seafood selections, chicken, and steak. The appetizers feature cheese-stuffed jalapenos. ($$)

MUSIC CITY GRILLE

(Near Broadway at the Beach) Formerly known as the Alabama Grille, Music City Grille is located on US 17 Bypass, across from Broadway at the Beach. The members of the musical group Alabama, Randy, Teddy, Jeff, and Mark, got their start in Myrtle Beach. The displays at this restaurant show off their pictures, guitars, signatures, framed outfits, sheet music, and favorite meals. While the memorabilia does focus on Alabama, the entire restaurant has a country music theme.

The menu is hearty and some of the favorites include bacon and cheese skins, Southern fried chicken salad, smokehouse burger, and the Alabama savory sirloin. ($$)

KYOTO JAPANESE STEAK HOUSE
(Broadway at the Beach, US 17 N ☎ 843.449.9294) Regardless of what you pick – chicken, beef, or seafood, and vegetables - are all chopped and cooked in front of you hibachi-style. The chef wows diners at the table with knife juggling and other tricks. All entrees are served with salad and onion soup. There's also a sushi bar for the adventurous. There are two locations, one at Broadway at the Beach, and the other in Murrells Inlet. Kyoto's serves dinner only and reservations are strongly suggested since the line here can get pretty long.

JOE'S CRAB SHACK
(Broadway at the Beach, 1219 Celebrity Circle ☎ 843.626.4490 ⌁ joescrabshack.com) The exterior looks tacky and the interior reminds one of a fishing camp. As the name indicates, crabs are on the menu year round – prepared and served in a number of different ways. Like them steamed, barbecued, or garlic style? It's all here. All kinds of crab varieties are served here, depending on the season.

You can choose to eat out on the patio or inside, where newspapers cover the tables. In case crabs aren't your thing, the menu does have other appetizers, sandwiches, salads, and steaks. There's a children's menu – "Rug Rats" – and a separate groups menu. Dress is casual. ($$)

BROADWAY LOUIE'S GRILL
(Broadway at the Beach ☎ 843.444.3500 ⌁ celebrationsnitelife.com/louie.htm) Broadway Louie's Grill boasts 12,000 square feet of space devoted to interactive video games, more than four dozen large screen TVs, the Karaoke Big Show, and extremely comfortable couches. There are many video arcade and skill games, including the Star Wars trilogy, Jurassic Park's Lost

World, Rapid Rivers, and Daytona 2. There's a pool table and each table has access to a trivia game.

The grill serves subs, appetizers, and New York-style pizza - hand-tossed and fresh from the oven. Open starting at noon. All ages are welcome, making it a family-friendly place

FUN STORES

The kinds of stores at Broadway at the Beach are not for the bargain-hunter or like a neighborhood mall. Merchandise is generally expensive, and geared, naturally, towards the tourist. Following are a few particularly interesting shops at Broadway at the Beach. Of course, there are many more stores than are listed here – anybody walking around is sure to find something of interest.

RIVER STREET SWEETS
(Broadway at the Beach ☎ *843.448.0962)* This Savannah, Georgia-based sweet shop has a store in Broadway at the Beach. The shop sells hand-dipped (and hand-made) pralines made with cream, butter, sugar, and pecan halves. The creamy caramel and milk chocolate bear claws are the store's best-selling chocolate treat. Several kinds of fudge line the display case in the back. The biggest draw, however, is the shop's salt water taffy, made from scratch. From outside, you can see the old-fashioned taffy machine – over 80 years old - that the staff uses to stretch the taffy. You can watch as the taffy is pulled by hand and stretched. Over 24 flavors are sold, and can be purchased in a mix-and-match.

ANYTHING JOE'S
(Broadway at the Beach ☎ *843.626.7141* ✆ *anythingjoes.com)* The shop specializes in personalized gifts for children. The gifts are personalized by painting, not by embroidery, and are available

for children of all ages. Along with the signature item, hand-painted classic piggy banks, the shop sells pillowcases, school bags, dance bags, backpacks, purses and totes. There are also door signs, bulletin boards and step stools.

NIGHTLIFE

Broadway at the Beach really heats up at night – the bars and clubs come alive, and many restaurants are converted into chic nightspots. On busy summer weekends, it is crowded with rowdy youngsters looking for a good time. This section describes nightlife specific to the Broadway at the Beach complex; for other nightlife options, see elsewhere in this guide.

CLUB BOCA
(Celebrity Square, Broadway at the Beach ☎ 843.444.3500 ⌘ celebrationsnitelife.com/boca.htm) DJs play mainstream and Latin dance tunes at this club, evoking a mix of Miami and Vegas. While partygoers must be 21 and over to get in, Club Boca also has "College Night" – allowing the under-21-but-over-18 crowd to come in and party. Open till late, the club is open every night.

REVOLUTIONS RETRO DANCE CLUB
(Broadway at the Beach ☎ 843.444.8032 ⌘ celebrationsnitelife.com) Featuring songs from the 70s, 80s, 90s, and "Beyond", Revolutions has both DJs and live bands. The club also shows music videos. There is a kitchen serving food. Open everyday from April to October, Revolutions is open only a few nights a week for the rest of the year. Cover charge varies by day of the week and whether a band is playing. The fee also allows you entry into Crocodile Rocks Dueling Pianos, located directly across Celebrity Square.

CROCODILE ROCKS DUELING PIANOS SALOON

(Broadway at the Beach, 1318 Celebrity Circle ☎ *843.444.2096)* As the name indicates, this show features dueling pianos. Two grand pianos face each other on a stage. Alternating players pound the keys all night. Requests (accompanied with cash) for songs are usually accommodated.

Audiences usually enjoy the bawdy renditions of songs being played. Patrons are often called up on stage to sing along, or act out the lyrics to the tune being played. At other times, the patrons on stage become targets for various jokes or join a skit. Some of the skits are off-color and may be inappropriate for children.

Crocodile Rocks is usually packed on weekends. Doors open at 7; pianos start at 8 pm. Admission fees are usually higher on weekends. There is a kitchen on premises, as well.

The admission fee here also gives you entry into the Revolutions Retro Dance Club across Celebrity Circle.

FROGGY BOTTOMZ

(Celebrity Square, Broadway at the Beach ☎ *843.444.3500* ⌘ *celebrationsnitelife.com/froggy.htm)* The complex offers live entertainment, current Top-40 tunes, oldies, and Latin music. The in-house band, Illuzions, knows all the popular tunes of the day. Also an over-21 club, College Night once a week welcomes the over-18 crowd. The club is open Fridays and Saturdays.

MALIBU'S SURF BAR

(Celebrity Square, Broadway at the Beach ☎ *843.444.3500* ⌘ *celebrationsnitelife.com/malibu.htm)* With a gigantic shark in the backdrop, the club is usually packed with dancers dancing to Top 40 music. The schedule and fees frequently change; call ahead.

Accommodations

Over 14 million visitors come to Myrtle Beach every year, and every single one of them needs a place to stay. The city has hotels, condominiums, resorts, motels, bed-and-breakfasts, and houses available for rent to accommodate the influx of visitors. While there are many places vying with each other to provide a roof over your vacationing head, don't be overconfident. Reservations are a must in this town – especially in the summer. Driving around looking for accommodations is not fun, especially if you arrive late in the evening or during the busy season. In fact, despite having so many rooms, many places are packed full during the high season.

Accommodation Prices:		
$	=	< $95
$$	=	$95 - $120
$$$	=	$121 - $150
$$$$	=	$150 - $175
$$$$$	=	> $175

When it comes to accommodations, the season begins in the spring, peaks in the summer, and falls in autumn. During the off-season – fall and winter - most places offer steep discounts to fill up their vacancies. Snowbirds – Northerners who fly south for the winter – can take advantage of these low rates.

In the past, most businesses – attractions as well as lodgings – were closed between Labor Day and Easter. The city now has enough visitors and snowbirds in the winter to keep these businesses open. If you are arriving after Labor Day, call ahead to confirm that the establishment is not closed for the winter.

The majority of the accommodations are located parallel to the beach, on Ocean Boulevard. The easternmost street in the city, it used to be considered the heart of the business district. With more development inland, and businesses moving to Broadway at the Beach, hotels are also opening off the main drag. The north end of town is considered to be more exclusive and prestigious. Many of the hotels and resorts in that part of town will play up the proximity to Restaurant Row.

For the hotels on Ocean Boulevard, all the rooms promise views of the ocean. Rooms can be either oceanfront or oceanview. Oceanfront properties are on the east side of Ocean Boulevard, on the beach. Oceanview properties, on the other hand, have a view of the ocean but aren't on the beach – such as being on the west side of Ocean Boulevard, or across the street from the beach. Sideview refers to rooms with either a balcony or walkway. Some properties list rooms that are next to a pool as poolside, as opposed to streetside.

Most hotels in the downtown area will not allow pets in the rooms; city law prohibits animals in public from March to September. It doesn't matter if your animal companion is on a leash or in a carrier. If your pet must accompany you on the trip, try to get a hotel outside the downtown area. Check to see if the hotel will allow your pet before making the reservation.

Most places require a deposit (usually on the credit card) at the time reservations are made. The deposit is usually credited towards your bill and is usually equal to the cost of one day's stay. Some places will accept cash or traveler's checks. Try to avoid using personal checks, since most local branches will not cash out-of-town personal checks unless you have an account with the bank.

When making a reservation, make sure to provide the time you plan to arrive. If you are arriving late, you don't want the hotel to give your room away, assuming you are a no-show. If you are planning to stay a week or later, many of the same places will offer a ten-percent discount. Ask about discounts. Along with the ten percent for long stays, most places offer senior citizen, travel club (such as AAA), and group discounts, as well.

Most of the accommodations in this chapter are wheelchair accessible. Visa and MasterCard are accepted; ask about other credit cards and other methods of payment when making the reservation. If you are interested in renting property for the duration of your stay, a list of rental agencies is provided at the end of the chapter.

The categories used in this chapter are, for the most part, arbitrary. The complete list is long and unwieldy. Most people have a general idea of what they want – a basic room to keep bags and sleep in, a luxurious resort packed with all kinds of amenities, or something in between. While there is a clear distinction between motels and hotels, the line is a bit blurry between hotels and resorts. The inns, for the most part, provide some form of dining option on premises.

Each listing has a dollar sign key and a list of packages the hotel can arrange at the end of the list. The dollar sign key used in this section is based on the "average" room rate for two people – usually with two double beds – per night in the middle of July. Since July is the peak of the summer season, you can assume the prices are lower than the key indicates during other times of the year. Also, weekends and holidays are always more expensive than during the week. The average is calculated by looking at all types of rooms available on that particular property.

INNS WITH THE PERSONAL TOUCH

In a place like Myrtle Beach, smaller hotels and inns are a dime a dozen, and easily discovered using online portals such as Travelocity or Hotels.com. There, however, go a bit beyond the standard fare.

DRIFTWOOD LODGE
(1600 North Ocean Blvd ☎ *843.448.1544* ✆ *driftwoodlodge.com)*
Driftwood Lodge is one of Myrtle Beach's original oceanfront

locations. Driftwood featured simple cottages 75 years ago; now Driftwood features three buildings and 90 rooms and suites.

This family-owned-and-operated lodge has large rooms ranging from 364 square feet to 887 square feet in size. Most rooms have private balconies and an ocean view. Many rooms are equipped with efficiency kitchens, including electric range and all utensils. In addition, there are extra-large suites, connecting rooms, and two penthouse suites.

The golf packages include lodging, breakfast, green fees, and golf cart. Some packages include courses. Play includes courses at Myrtle Beach National. ($$, golf)

SEA ISLAND INN ON THE BEACH

(6000 North Ocean Blvd ☎ 843.449.6406 ✆ seaislandonthebeach.com)
Sea Island offers guests a full breakfast and a five-course dinner in the hotel dining room. The dining room serves breakfast and dinner, with some lunch options out on the patio and at the pool bar in the summer.

The hotel has 1113 oceanfront units, with one, two, three, and four bedroom suites. The suites, decorated with a Tropical British West Indies flare, have full kitchens (with granite counter tops), large living room, and a TV and private bath in each bedroom. All suites come with high speed internet access, a washer and dryer, cable TV, DVD player or a VCR, and a balcony overlooking the ocean. Some of the larger units have Jacuzzi tubs, separate shower, and a walk-in closet.

In operation since 1981, the owners extensively upgraded the facility in 2004. Reconstruction ended in 2006, and the Sea Island Inn held its grand re-opening in May 2006, in time for the busy season. The new hotel features architecture reminiscent of Howard Mizner and south Florida in the 1930s.

The hotel has an indoor/outdoor pool complex. Many of the features are closed in the winter. The lazy river, enclosed in the cooler months, has rock walls with cascading waterfalls. There are three pools, a splash pool and slide for the children, and spas. A beautiful manicured lawn adjacent to the complex is a popular summer picnic spot and sunbathing. The hotel also has an indoor fitness center equipped with treadmills, cardio machines, and weight stations.

During the summer, the hotel offers supervised activities, including poolside games, scavenger hunts, pizza and movie nights, and arts and crafts. Golfers can choose courses to play from amongst thirty courses spread out over the area. ($$$)

HOLIDAY INN AT THE PAVILION

(1200 North Ocean Blvd ☎ *800.211.7143* *myrtlebeach-resorts.com)* The Holiday Inn at the Pavilion is not part of the nationwide budget chain with the same name. Instead, it is a sister resort to Sea Crest and Coral Beach, both a few blocks south. The name comes from the amusement park Pavilion, which closed in 2006.

There are oceanfront rooms, suites, and efficiencies, and ocean view rooms and efficiencies. They all have private balconies. Each unit has a microwave and refrigerator.

This resort has five pools: children's activity pool, indoor whirlpool, indoor pool, an outdoor pool, and an indoor lazy river. Tropical Paradise Beach Bar is an oceanfront pool bar serving cold and mixed drinks. A complimentary deluxe continental breakfast is served daily.

Guests have access to an exercise room and laundry services. Tennis players can play on the courts at the private club nearby. Guests also have access to some of the facilities at Sea Crest and Coral Beach resorts.

SERENDIPITY INN

(407 71 Avenue N ☎ *843.449.5268* *serendipityinn.com)* The Spanish mission style inn is located at the north end of Myrtle Beach,

off a quiet residential street. The inn offers guests separate entrances and a continental breakfast in the garden room. The bed & breakfast has fifteen units, which range from a single room to a king suite, which has three rooms. The central courtyard has a private pool, hot tub, shuffleboard, table tennis, and bicycles. ($$)

Resorts

The following resorts are fairly standard for Myrtle Beach. They offer oceanfront apartments, suites, and condos. What set them apart are the little things that they offer in addition to a place to sleep, a place to swim and play, and a place to eat.

BEACH COLONY RESORT

(5308 North Ocean Blvd ☎ 843.449.4010 ✆ beachcolony.com) This resort has approximately 220 units with seven different room layouts, including oceanfront two-, three-, and four- bedroom apartments, oceanfront suites, and oceanview studios. All suites have a private balcony, a fully equipped kitchen and a living area with a sleeper sofa.

There are two heated outdoor pools, an outdoor whirlpool, an indoor pool, an indoor whirlpool, a heated kiddie pool, a lazy river, a video arcade, a sauna, racquetball courts, guest laundry facilities, an oceanfront lounge, a pool bar, an exercise room, and an Italian restaurant on the premises. An exercise trail and tennis courts are nearby. The resort has an on-site golf director for golfers, and a children's activity program in season.

The oceanfront restaurant, Fusco's, serves breakfast and dinner specials along with views of the ocean. The pool bar is a combination snack bar, grill, and ice cream parlor, serving frozen drinks and a light menu such as hamburgers, hot dogs and sandwiches. The Ocean Lounge serves drinks and a light menu.

The Beach Colony Resort specializes in small to mid-size groups - motorcoaches, churches, associations, corporations, military and social. Meeting rooms are available for group events.

The staff can assist in arranging reservations for restaurants, shows, sight-seeing tours, and golf-tee-times. ($$$, golf packages, show packages)

BREAKERS RESORT HOTEL TOWER

(2006 North Ocean Blvd ☎ *843.444.4444* 🖱 *breakers.com)* Only three blocks from the convention center, this resort is made up of three buildings: The Breakers New Paradise Tower, The Breakers Resort Hotel, and The Breakers Boutique North Tower. Regardless of which tower you stay in, you can take advantage of the amenities at all three resorts.

The Breakers Resort Hotel is central of the three, and features oceanfront rooms and suites. Amenities include an oceanfront lawn, multiple pools and whirlpools, an indoor pool and whirlpool, exercise room, restaurant and meeting facilities that can accommodate groups of up to 150 people.

The oceanfront Paradise Tower is adjacent to The Breakers Resort Hotel and features one- two- and three- bedroom condominiums with enclosed corridors, an oceanfront water park with a 418-foot lazy river, several pools and whirlpools. The waterpark has a kiddie play area. Enclosed in the winter, the park is accessible year round.

The North Tower is, you guessed it, north of The Breakers Resort Hotel, and features one, two, and three-room suites. The North Tower has an oceanfront pool, an extra-large kiddie pool, a whirlpool, and a well-equipped excrcise room.

Breakers offers golf packages that include room and tee times at select courses. Packages with afternoon tee times tend to be cheaper. Some courses offer packages that offer a free round of golf depending on the length of stay. Breakers can arrange play on several courses, including Arrowhead Country Club, Blackmoor Golf Club, Grande Dunes, Myrtle Beach National, Legends, Man O' War Golf, Myrtlewood Golf, Pine Lakes International Country Club, Prestwick Country Club, and Wizard, among others.

Breakers also offers several packages and discounts. The Starbucks Weekender includes coffee and pastry from the shop. Holiday show packages include tickets to shows. Bed and breakfast packages include breakfast buffets. Discounts are available to AAA and AAARP members. ($$$$, golf package)

CORAL BEACH RESORT & SUITES
(1105 South Ocean Blvd ☎ 800.556.1754 ✆ thecoralbeach.com) Coral Beach Resort & Suites is easily recognizable by the covered passenger walkway across Ocean Boulevard connecting the hotel with the parking lot across the street. Guests can walk from their car to the resort without having to deal with traffic.

The rooms have private balconies, refrigerators, and microwaves. Suites and efficiencies also include a range and oven and a full sized refrigerator. Along with a range, cookware and dinnerware are provided.

The resort has ten pools: two outdoor pools, two outdoor kiddie pools, a Lazy river, an indoor heated pool, an outdoor Jacuzzi, and three indoor Jacuzzis. The on-site recreation center offers eight bowling lanes, and a video arcade. The recreation center also has a game room with pool tables, air hockey, and foosball.

The resort offers live entertainment such as karaoke parties. Comedians perform at the MacDivot's Sports Pub and the Comedy Corner on Wednesday, Thursday, Friday, and Saturday evenings.

While there is a snack bar and grill in the recreation center, the Atlantic Marketplace features a variety of specialty cafes. Sandbunker's Beach Bar and Grill serves meals and drinks.

The general store and gift shop stocks basic necessities and more. Guests have access to the fitness center, children's activity center, meeting facilities, laundry services, and men and women's saunas. Tennis players can play on the courts at the private club nearby. The staff will help make arrangements for water sports such as kayaking and renting a banana boat.

Coral Beach offers four kinds of golf packages to fit your budget and skill level: Custom Classic, Signature Club Collection, The Royal Tour, Economy Golf Getaway. Packages include room, green fees, and daily breakfast.

Discounts to amusement parks are available in family packages, which includes an angle-oceanfront efficiency, unlimited daily passes for the whole family (up to five people) to Family Kingdom Water Park, two all-day park passes to Family Kingdom Amusement Park (go-carts excluded), four rounds of miniature golf, and unlimited bowling at the recreation center. Children 16 years old and younger get free breakfasts as part of the package. ($$$$$, golf packages, amusement parks)

HILTON MYRTLE BEACH RESORT

(10000 Beach Club Dr ☏ *843.449.5000)* The resort offers 385 rooms and suites, each with a private balcony overlooking the ocean. Units have whirlpools and fireplaces. Wireless Internet access is available for a fee.

There are two heated indoor and two heated outdoor pools, whirlpool, and oceanfront pool deck. Supervised children's activities are scheduled poolside during the summer.

The hotel has two restaurants: Café Almalfi for casual fine dining, and Beachcomber's Restaurant for casual dining. The oceanfront Café Almalfi serves breakfast, lunch, dinner, and

Sunday brunch. Beachcomber's is poolside, serving sandwiches. Wet Whistle Pool Bar serves drinks. The Veranda Bar and The Bakery offer snacks. Once you step out of the hotel, you can play golf at Arcadian Shores, an 18-hole 72-par championship golf course. Guests get reduced green fees and lessons.

You can also stroll over to Kingston Plantation to play tennis at The Sport and Health Club, splash around at Splash! Waterpark, or try other water sports and beach volleyball. Boating and fishing are also available. ($$$$, golf, romance, weddings)

KINGSTON PLANTATION
(kingstonplantation.com) Sprawling over 145 acres, Kingston Plantation has 1300 units extending across its properties, namely the Hilton Myrtle Beach Resort at Arcadian Shores golf course, the Embassy Suites Hotel, and Myrtle Beach Condos.

"SPLASH!" is the resort's on-site waterpark, open from Memorial Day to Labor Day. The Caribbean Water Playground has water slides, waterspouts, arch jet sprays and a 500-gallon bucket that dumps water onto participants below. SPLASH! has two large swimming pools, two kiddie pools, lazy river and three Jacuzzis. There are also supervised children's activities scheduled during the season. The pool area has lounge chairs and beach towels for adults. Poolside waitstaff bring you tropical drinks and food off the menu. The Sports and Health Club has nine lighted tennis courts and racquetball courts.

For food, the resort has two oceanfront restaurants, an oceanfront lounge, and an outdoor Splash Café (open in the summer).

Embassy Suites Hotel offers 255 oceanview and oceanfront two room suites. Each suite is appointed with either two double beds or a king bed and each suite features a living area and a private balcony. Wireless Internet access is available for a fee.

Guests get a complimentary breakfast buffet and an evening reception.

The Hilton Myrtle Beach Resort offers 385 guestrooms with private balconies, two oceanfront restaurants, and a snack bar. Wireless Internet access is available for a nominal fee. All rooms include a microwave and mini refrigerator. A complimentary newspaper is delivered to the room every morning.

The condos are in four towers: Brighton, North Hampton, South Hampton, and Margate. Brighton Tower features one-, two-, and three-bedroom oceanfront and oceanview condominiums. Margate Tower features two-, three-, and four-bedroom oceanfront and oceanview condominiums. North Hampton features two-, and three-bedroom oceanfront and oceanview condominiums. South Hampton features one-bedroom guest rooms, two-bedroom oceanview and oceanfront condominiums, and three-bedroom oceanview condominiums. Special winter rental rates are available. Myrtle Beach Villas and two-bedroom split-level Town homes and Lodges are also available in the winter. ($$$$, golf, romance, weddings)

THE PALACE RESORT
(1605 S. Ocean Blvd ☎ 843.448.4300 ◌ palaceresort.com) The Palace features one- and two-bedroom condos and oceanfront suites with a fully-equipped kitchen and living room area. The Palace rents to only couples and families.

The Palace Resort has a putting green, an indoor pool, several outdoor pools, spas, and an exercise room. There's also a lounge and restaurant on premises. Anyone can work out in the exercise room. Guests have access to the bowling alley at the recreation center at nearby Captain's Quarters in the spring, fall, and winter. Each room gets one hour of free bowling each day.

Golf packages include playing 18 holes of golf, room, and breakfast. Carts are not included. A deposit per person is required to confirm tee times, which are guaranteed. Changing or canceling tee times for a foursome require 72 hour notice; 15 days for groups of 20 or more. ($$$, golf packages)

SEA CREST OCEANFRONT RESORT
(803 South Ocean Blvd ☎ 888.889.8113 ⌁ gotomyrtle.com) Regardless of the layout, each room at Sea Crest Oceanfront Resort has private balconies and offer views of the ocean. There are oceanfront suites and efficiencies, sideview rooms and efficiencies, and Jacuzzi suites.

Sea Crest has eight pools: a children's activity pool with "Freddie the Frog" and rain-maker, two indoor Jacuzzis, an indoor pool, an outdoor pool, an indoor lazy river, an outdoor lazy river, and a baby pool.

The Malibu's Beach Bar has live entertainment shows during the day and karaoke at night. Surf's Up Deli is right in the pool area. A luau is held on the lawn on Sunday and Wednesday evenings during the summer.

A mini-mart and gift shop stock most basic necessities and other items for your convenience. A complimentary deluxe continental breakfast is served daily. Guests also have access to an exercise room, laundry services, and a concierge. Guests also have access to the recreation center at Coral Beach, two blocks south. Each reservation is good for two free games. Tennis players can play on the courts at the private club nearby

Sea Crest offers four kinds of golf packages to fit your budget and skill level: Custom Classic, Signature Club Collection, The Royal Tour, Economy Golf Getaway. Packages include room, green fees, and daily breakfast. Courses include Prestwick, The Wizard, World Tour, and many others.

Discounts to amusement parks are available in family packages, which includes an angle-oceanfront efficiency, unlimited daily passes for the whole family (up to five people) to Family

Kingdom Water Park, two all-day park passes to Family Kingdom Amusement Park (go-carts excluded), four rounds of miniature golf, and unlimited bowling at the recreation center. Children 16 years old and younger get free breakfasts as part of the package. ($$$$$, golf packages, amusement parks)

SEA MIST OCEANFRONT RESORT
(1200 South Ocean Blvd. ☎ *800.793.6507* 🖱 *myrtlebeachseamist.com)*
A fifteen-acre oceanfront property, Sea Mist features 823 rooms, efficiencies, suites, townhouses, and bungalows with new bathrooms and kitchens. The kitchen has new appliances. Some of the suites are Jacuzzi suites.

The property has several on-site restaurants. Tena's Restaurant serves a 46-item breakfast buffet and special dinner events. Pete & Polly's Parrot-Ice is located in the water park. Jason's Café & Ice Cream Parlor serves wraps, salads, flying kids meals, and boulevard burgers. Kids also enjoy the doughnut shop. Guests relax in the Lighthouse Lounge and the Barefoot Cabana offer refreshments and live entertainment from mid-April to August.

An on-site arcade has over 120 videogames. Misty Falls Miniature Golf runs through August. Guests have access to a fitness center.

The resort's water park is exclusive to Sea Mist guests. It opens in Mid-March and closes late in the season, long after all other parks have closed. It is open every single night until 9pm during the summer. The 670 foot long lazy river is heated when necessary in March, April and October. The lazy river has mini water slides. The park also has a wading pool, BooBoo the Bear water swing, a dolphin slide, an otter slide, a mushroom rain tree, a three-story high tubular speed slide and multiple sundecks. The Children's Activity Pool has a dinosaur slide, a whale slide, rain tree, and more sundecks. There are ten pools

The resort specializes in family vacation packages, championship golf, shows, attractions, and amusements. The Family Value package includes tickets to the Family Kingdom Oceanfront Water Park every single day. Discount tickets are available through the Activities Desk. ($$, golf, attractions)

SHERATON MYRTLE BEACH CONVENTION CENTER HOTEL 🌟

(2101 North Oak St ☎ 843.918.5000) The hotel is attached to the Myrtle Beach Convention Center and is in the city's central business district. The hotel has 402 units, including junior suites, executive suites, and club suites, each with a private balcony. Each room provides high-speed internet access (for a fee) and work stations with an ergonomic desk chair. The living room has a sofa bed and a television with Internet access and a wireless keyboard (the Internet access is also for a fee).

The hotel provides plush robes and is famous for its seven layers of down bedding in each room. Club members and Starwood Preferred Guests have private, keyed access floors with upgraded amenities. Non-smoking rooms are also available.

Guests have access to an indoor heated pool, a fitness facility, a sun deck, and a whirlpool. There is a limited airport shuttle service. There's also a car rental service on premises.

Laundry/valet service is available, as well as business center and a gift shop. There's also an ATM. Vidalia's Restaurant, the hotels' full-service restaurant, is open for breakfast, lunch, and dinner and serves southern, low-country specialties. The M-Bar offers cocktails and light fare. Complimentary wireless access is available at the bar. Coffee & Cream serves coffee, bagel, or other light items for breakfast and lunch. Wireless is also available there. ($$$)

SANDS RESORTS

(☎ 800.726.3783 ⌁ sandsresorts.com) The Sands Resorts in Myrtle Beach is a collection of six oceanfront resorts. Though the resorts themselves are separate, and have separate amenities and activities, they all share the same corporate parent. The properties that are part of Sands Resorts give a feeling of staying at a place bigger than one property. Guests at one resort can eat and play at any of the sister resorts, so there are more choices. Overall, these are large properties with oodles of resort goodness.

The Sands Resorts first opened its doors in 1972 with a mere 150 guest rooms. The resort now has six oceanfront properties with 1,640 available guest rooms, which accommodate over 4,000 guests. The holding company has an interest in the Legends golf course, which gives guests special privileges at that course. The following places are part of Sands Resorts: Ocean Dunes Resort and Villas, Ocean Forest Plaza, Ocean Forest Villa, Sands Beach Club, Sand Dunes Resort, Sands Ocean Club.

The Sands Privilege Card from the Sands Resort you are staying at covers admission to the Sands Waterpark at Sand Dunes Resort and Ocean Dunes Resort. The card can also be used to "charge" your meals at other restaurants. The cost is charged to your room.

Sands has several programs for children. Children 12 years and under eat breakfast for free at the resort. Children 18 years and under stay for free if they are with their parents. From Memorial Day to Labor Day, the Kids Club programs children's activities.

Guests at any of the six properties have access to the Sands Waterpark at Sand Dunes and Ocean Dunes, and the Sands Health Club. The waterpark includes waterslides, a waterfall, a lazy river, and a bubble pool. The park is open daily during the summer, with shorter days in September. In October, the park will be open only in the afternoons on Friday, Saturday, and Sunday.

The health club, located at Ocean Dunes Resort & Villas, features strength-training and cardiovascular exercise equipment, steam room, sauna, whirlpool, heated indoor and outdoor pool, and massage therapy. Professional trainers are on hand to work with you. Guests can also receive relaxing and therapeutic spa treatments such as the Swedish and deep tissue massages. Bicycles are available for rent. Golfers can play at over 100 championship golf courses, including the resort's Legends Golf Course. Tennis players can play on the courts at Sands Beach. Children have access to the playground and water play area at Sand Dunes.

OCEAN DUNES RESORT AND VILLAS
(205 75th Ave N ☎ 843.449.7441 ⁂ sandsresorts.com) Part of the Sands Resorts, this resort features 400 rooms in a variety of suites, efficiencies, villas and penthouses. Each unit has a view of the ocean, a refrigerator, and a microwave. Non-smoking units are available.

Ocean Dunes has two indoor and five outdoor pools, and seven whirlpools. Children have access to a playground and a water play area. Banana's Game room is also on premises.

The Sands Waterpark and Sands Health Club are both located on this resort. The waterpark features waterslides, a waterfall, a lazy river, and a bubble pool. Open daily during the summer, the park has reduced hours in September, and is open only in the afternoons on Friday, Saturday, and Sunday in October. The health club features strength-training and cardiovascular exercise equipment, steam room, sauna, whirlpool, heated indoor pool and massage therapy.

A wholesale golf shop is stocked with basic necessities and essentials. Guests can choose to either take advantage of the same-day laundry and valet service or use the coin-operated laundry machines. There's an ATM on premises.

There are several restaurants at Ocean Dunes. Brass Anchor Food 'N' Drink serves breakfast buffet and dinner. Brass Anchor Lounge has happy hour specials daily. The Little Nassau Pool Bar serves a wide selection of drinks.

The resort plans outdoor events, cookouts, and family activities all through the summer.

Guests staying at Ocean Dunes have guest privileges at all Sands Resorts. Please refer to the listing for Sands Resorts for more details. ($$$$, golf packages, entertainment packages)

OCEAN FOREST PLAZA

(5523 N Ocean Blvd ☎ 843.497.0044 ✆ sandsresorts.com) Part of the Sands Resorts, Ocean Forest Plaza features one-, two- and three-bedroom suites. Each suite has a view of the ocean, a refrigerator, and a microwave. The living room has a sleeper sofa.

Ocean Forest Plaza has a sauna, an indoor pool and whirlpool and a heated outdoor pool. Children have access to a nearby playground. Guests can also use the coin-operated laundry machines. Tennis players can play at a nearby private club.

There are several restaurants at Ocean Forest Plaza. Ocean Forest Cafe serves breakfast. The Plaza Club Lounge and Grille and Forest Plaza Pool Bar serve snacks and drinks. The Summer Beach Party Grill has cookouts Wednesdays through Saturdays during the summer season.

Guests staying at Ocean Forest Plaza have access to the health club, waterpark, and other restaurants at its sister resorts. See the listing for Sands Resorts for more details.

Motorcycles are not allowed at this resort. ($$$$, golf packages, entertainment packages)

OCEAN FOREST VILLAS

(5601 N Ocean Blvd ☎ 843.449.9661 ⌂ sandsresorts.com) Part of the Sands Resorts, all the units in Ocean Forest Villas are two-bedroom condos with private balconies overlooking the ocean. Each condo has two bathrooms, a standard living room, dining area and a full-sized, fully-equipped kitchen. The living room has a sleeper sofa.

Ocean Forest Villas has two outdoor pools, two heated whirlpools, and a kiddie pool. Tennis players can play at a nearby private club. Children can play at a nearby playground.

Guests can choose to either take advantage of the same-day laundry and valet service or use the coin-operated laundry machines.

Guests staying at Sands Beach have access to the health club, waterpark, and other restaurants at its sister resorts. See the listing for Sands Resorts for more details.

Motorcycles are not allowed on this property. ($$$$, golf packages, entertainment packages)

SANDS BEACH CLUB

(9400 Shore Dr ☎ 843.449.1531 ⌂ sandsresorts.com) Part of the Sands Resorts, this oceanfront resort features one- and two-bedroom suites. Each room has a view of the ocean, a refrigerator, and a microwave.

Sands Beach Club has an indoor pool, an outdoor pool, a kiddie pool, and a whirlpool for its guests. There is a Sports Deck with basketball and volleyball courts and lighted tennis courts. The outdoor grill area can be used for cookouts.

Guests can choose to either take advantage of the same-day laundry and valet service or to use the coin-operated laundry machines. There's an ATM on premises.

Sands Beach has several eating options. Topper's Oceanfront Restaurant offers a casual fine dining experience. California Pizza serves Italian subs and pizza. A full-service restaurant, Cafe Havana serves breakfast, and Cadillac Bar is a lounge. There's also a poolside lounge.

Guests staying at Sands Beach have access to the health club, waterpark, and other restaurants at its sister resorts. See the listing for Sands Resorts for more details. ($$$$, golf packages, entertainment packages)

SAND DUNES RESORT

(201 74th Ave N ☎ 843.449.3313 ⌁ sandsresorts.com) Part of the Sands Resorts, this oceanfront resort features 400 guest accommodations ranging from hotel rooms to one, two, & three bedroom executive suites. Each room has a refrigerator and microwave, and private balconies. High speed Internet access is available.

Sand Dunes Resort has an indoor and outdoor pool, lazy rivers, a whirlpool, a children's playground and water play area.

A convenience store stocks basic necessities. Guests can choose to either take advantage of the same-day laundry and valet service or to use the coin-operated laundry machines. There's an ATM on premises.

Sand Dunes has several eating options. Mango's Restaurant serves a breakfast buffet and Caribbean themed dinners. California Pizza is also on the premises. It serves Italian subs and pizza. Mango's Lounge is a sports bar.

Guests staying at Sand Dunes have access to the health club, waterpark, and other restaurants at its sister resorts. See the listing for Sands Resorts for more details. ($$$$, golf packages, entertainment packages)

SANDS OCEAN CLUB

(9550 Shore Dr ☏ *843.449.6461* ⌕ *sandsresorts.com)* Part of the Sands Resorts, Sands Ocean Club Resort features 450 rooms, suites, efficiencies and executive suites. Each unit has a refrigerator and microwave, and private balconies with views of the ocean. High speed Internet access is available in each unit.

The resort has indoor and outdoor pools, a lazy river, and a whirlpool. There's an exercise room for guests and a game room. A wholesale golf shop, a gift shop, and a convenience store are stocked with basic necessities and essentials. Guests can choose to either take advantage of the same-day laundry or valet service or to use the coin-operated laundry machines. There's an ATM on premises.

The Atlantis Spa offers a variety of treatments, including massage therapy, sugar scrubs, facials, foot massages, manicures, and pedicures.

Sands Ocean has several dining options. Window's Oceanfront Restaurant serves breakfast daily. Sandal's Lounge serves cocktails and offers entertainment and daily happy hours. During the summer, there is Ocean Annie's - an outdoor beach bar with live music and tropical drinks.

Guests staying at Sands Ocean have access to the health club, waterpark, and other restaurants at its sister resorts. See the listing for Sands Resorts for more details. ($$$$, golf packages, entertainment packages)

BROADWAY AT THE BEACH

The hotels in this section were selected because of their proximity to **Broadway at the Beach**. There are increasing numbers of properties springing up away from Ocean Boulevard and the beach. These properties by Broadway at the Beach means guests have easy access to various entertainment and dining venues.

HAMPTON INN MYRTLE BEACH - BROADWAY AT THE BEACH

(1140 Celebrity Circle ☎ *843.916.0600)* Located at Broadway at the Beach, the hotel has 141 standard rooms, king rooms or whirlpool suites. The rooms have high-speed Internet access. Local calls made from the room's telephone are free. There's also no extra surcharge for using a calling card. A copy of *USA Today* is delivered to each room every morning from Monday to Friday.

A complimentary deluxe continental breakfast is served daily. The hotel lobby has free wireless and complimentary coffee and tea. There's also an ATM.

This Hampton Inn has a swimming pool, a whirlpool, a fitness center, a business center (with a fax service), and meeting facilities. Audio-visual equipment is available for a fee. Both laundry valet services and a self-Laundromat are available. ($$$, golf packages)

HOLIDAY INN EXPRESS: BROADWAY AT THE BEACH

(1290 Paradise Circle ☎ *843.916.4993)* The Holiday Inn Express is adjacent to Broadway at the Beach. Last renovated in 1999, the property has 114 units, of which 18 are singles and 96 are doubles. A majority of the rooms are non-smoking. Free continental breakfast is served daily.

While pets are not allowed on premises, there are kennels nearby. The Holiday Inn Express can provide telephone numbers for the kennel to make advance reservations with the kennels. The kennels will charge a fee for the service. ($)

SHERATON BROADWAY PLANTATION

(3301 Robert M. Grissom Pkwy ☎ *843.916.8855)* The all-villa resort is adjacent to the Broadway at the Beach. Each one- or two-

bedroom villa has its own whirlpool, private patio, gourmet kitchens, and a spacious living area with a sofa bed. The resort offers car rental service and a children's program of scheduled activities. Guests have access to indoor and outdoor heated pools and sundeck. For children, there's a playground and a separate children's pool. A volleyball court, basketball court, fitness facility, a game room, and a miniature golf course are available. Sunnie's Poolside Bar & Grill serves light fare poolside. ($$$$)

DAYS INN MYRTLE BEACH

(3650 Waccamaw Blvd, Hwy 501 at River Oaks Dr. ☎ 843.236.9888 ✆ myrtlebeachdaysinn.com) Two miles from Broadway at the Beach and three miles from the beach, this Days Inn has 154 double rooms and efficiencies. Each room also has data ports. Some rooms have a microwave, refrigerator, and/or a sofa-bed. All local calls are free using the room telephone, and there are no additional access fees to make toll (1-800) or long distance calls.

Guests have access to an outdoor pool, hot tub, exercise room, and laundry facilities. The property also features a tropical courtyard with a gazebo. Toiletries are available upon request at the front desk. At the 24-hour Business Center, guests can make copies for free on the copy machine, print documents for free, and use a computer hooked up to the Internet for free.

The staff will arrange golf packages upon request. For guests looking to stay a while, extended stay rates are available. Each room receives a free newspaper in the morning. A deluxe continental breakfast is served.

Guests must be at least 18 years old and have picture ID to stay in a room unaccompanied by a parent or legal guardian. Guests between 18 and 25 years of age traveling without a parent of legal guardian are required to put down a damage deposit at check-in. ($, golf packages)

LA QUINTA INN AND SUITES

(1561 21 Avenue N ☎ 843.916.8801) Across the street from Broadway at the Beach, this property bucks the trend of cramming hotels along Ocean Boulevard. The property features 128 units, of which eight are suites. Each room has a telephone with a computer dataport, a refrigerator, a microwave oven, a coffeemaker, a television, and videogames. Some rooms have high-speed Internet access for free. All local calls made from the room's telephone are free. Guests receive a free copy of *USA Today* every morning.

La Quinta allows guests to bring small pets. Guests also have access to an outdoor heated pool, spa, and exercise room. Meeting facilities and an airport shuttle are also available. A complimentary deluxe continental breakfast is served daily. ($$)

RV AND CAMPGROUNDS

Each campground listed here offers basic services plus some recreational activities. While summer is the most popular time for camping, most campgrounds are open year-round. Advance reservations are recommended, even during the off-season, since many of the campgrounds can be full of campers taking advantage of the mild climate and cheap rates.

APACHE FAMILY CAMPGROUNDS

(9700 Kings Rd ☎ 843.449.7323 ⁂ apachefamilycampground.com) The campground has over 700 campsites, but less than half are available for rent. Most of the sites are annual rentals or permanently booked, giving the campground a feel of a neighborhood. Each campsite has sewage hookups, free cable TV, and picnic tables. The campground also has a large swimming pool, laundry facilities, and a fully stocked shop.

The sites are all within easy distance of the ocean. A courtesy patrol is available 24 hours a day. Arcade games, a playground, a diner, storage facilities, a dump station, and a picnic area is also available. The campground also offers propane and 50 amp power pedestals.

Pull-thru sites are also available. Pets are welcome at the campgrounds. The fishing pier, the widest and longest in the Southeast, is part of the campground. The pier has a restaurant and a lounge featuring live entertainment. ($)

LAKEWOOD CAMPING RESORT
(5901 South Kings Hwy ☎ 843.238.5161 ✍ lakewoodcampground.com) This campground is one of the largest in the area, with over 1000 campsites. The sites are either oceanfront, lakefront, or wooded. The sites are large enough to accommodate double slideouts. Pull-thru sites are also available. Pets are welcome on the campgrounds, as long as they are registered with the office during check-in. Pets are not allowed in villa rentals. Lakewood allows only "quiet, non-aggressive breeds."

The campground offers amenities including wi-fi, 62 channels of Time Warner cable TV, full-service bathhouses, and modern laundry facilities. The campground also has a dump station, 50, 30, 20 amp power pedestals, and propane delivery. Most of the sites have sewer connections. A picnic table is provided on each site. The campsites include a free telephone connection; all local calls made are free.

Personal generators are not permitted. The campground offers indoor and outdoor pools. There are waterslides, a miniature golf course, two playgrounds, shuffleboard, basketball, horseshoes, and volleyball. Five fresh-water lakes are stocked regularly.

From mid-June to mid-August children can join Sharkey's Kids Club for a fee and get pizza and a movie in the afternoon. The Kids Club also runs from mid-June to mid-August and meets at the Information Center in the mornings. From Memorial Day to Labor Day kids can get surf lessons (for a fee), a weekly magic show, and participate in flag football tournaments, putt-putt tournaments and boat races. The winter season is limited to ice cream socials, Bingo, potluck dinners, white flag shuffle, and bocce ball.

While campfires are permitted on the campsite, they are not allowed on the beach. The campground offers discounts, including reduced rates if more than seven nights are paid up in advance, and even deeper discounts if more than a month is paid up in advance. There are special discounts for the off-season, from January to April, and September through December. Senior citizen discounts – for people 55 and over – are also available. Reservations are accepted up to 18 months in advance. ($)

MYRTLE BEACH STATE PARK
(4401 South Kings Hwy ☏ 843.238.5325) The state park is just three miles south of downtown Myrtle Beach and has the first campground built in the area. The campground is less than 300 yards from the beach and has over 350 sites, picnic areas with shelters, a swimming pool, nature trails, a playground, a store, and a snack bar on the premises. Most of the sites are rented on a first-come-first-served basis; only a hundred are available for advance reservation, and it must be for a minimum of two nights.

The registration happens at the store, which is near the entrance. The store carries limited groceries, camping supplies, souvenirs, drinks, snacks, and firewood. If you are planning to arrive after the park is closed, contact the park office beforehand for the gate combination that will give access to the campgrounds. Each site has electricity and water. Laundromats, hot showers, and restrooms are easily accessible. There is a dump station.

While many of the sites can accommodate RVs up to 40 feet, most are for RVs up to 30 feet. There are plenty of sites for tents and smaller units. There's also a 45-site overflow campground, which is open only in June, July, and August, designated for tent camping. These sites have access to water, but no electricity. ($)

MYRTLE BEACH TRAVEL PARK

(10108 Kings Rd ☎ 843.449.3714 ⌘ myrtlebeachtravelpark.com) The travel park offers oceanfront campsites as well as wooded sites with oaks and lakeview sites on the bluffs.

Guests have access to modern laundry facilities, hot showers, a heated indoor pool and an outdoor pool, a complete grocery store, public telephones, a gift shop, a restaurant and snack bar, a recreation room, sanitary disposal stations, and a chapel. A resident campground chaplain holds services and various events during the summer.

Guests interested in fishing will enjoy the 17 acre freshwater lake stocked with bass and bream. The playground and other recreational areas have been landscaped. The campground provides liquid propane and year-round RV storage.

Each campsite has cable TV, sewer connections, and full utilities. The parking space has picnic tables. Pull thru level parking is also available. The sites also have wireless Internet. The electrical boxes can handle 110 plugs, standard 30 amp trailer plugs, and 50 amp connectors found on larger RV's. ($)

OCEAN LAKES FAMILY CAMPGROUND

(6001 South Kings Hwy ☎ 843.238.5636 ⌘ oceanlakes.com) Ocean Lakes claims to offer "5 star camping" with its many amenities.

The Ocean Lakes Family Campground has 893 sites. All sites are pull-thru and can accommodate a 40-foot camper with slideouts on both sides. Some sites are much larger. Each campsite features a cable hook-up featuring TV channels as long as you bring your own TV. All sites include water, sewer, electric, a modem-friendly phone jack with free local calls, daily curbside trash pickup, and a picnic table. Tents are welcome on all sites as well. There are also approximately 300 fully furnished beach houses and trailers available for rent. A security group patrols the campgrounds 24 hours a day.

Ocean Lakes' perimeter measures 3 miles and has about 29 miles of paved roads in the interior. The beach is about a mile long, with an observation deck and a concession area. Bicycles and electric golf cars are available for rent to get around the park.

Ocean Lakes has two pools, a sun deck, a poolside café, and a recreation center. Kids can splash in two kiddie pools, go to the games center or the nature center. "Kamp Starfish" is a program where the staff takes care of the children. The store sells bait for fishing in the surf or in the eight freshwater lakes on the property. The store also sells groceries, snacks, ice, gifts, and souvenirs. The laundry facilities also offer to wash and fold your clothes for you. Reservations are made up to 18 months in advance. ($)

PIRATELAND FAMILY CAMPGROUND

(5402 US 17 S ☎ *843.238.5155* ⌂ *pirateland.com)* The 140-acre oceanfront park has woodland and lakes. There are over a thousand campsites, each fully equipped with a picnic table, utility hookups, and free cable TV. Trailer storage space is available.

Two-three bedroom Lakeview Villas can be rented. The "executive" rentals are doublewide and have three bedrooms and two full baths. The two-bedroom villas have one full bathroom, and the three-bedroom villas has one bath-shower, but no tub. All the rentals have central air and heating, a fully equipped kitchen (including a coffeemaker and a microwave!), a modem accessible phone, a private deck, and cable TV. The tenants provide linens, blankets, pillows, towels, grills, and cleaning supplies.

There's a recreation center, a full Laundromat, 24-hour security patrol, hot showers, basketball courts, a heated indoor pool, bathhouses, and a propane pumping station. Golf cars and wheelchairs for the beach are available.

Surf fishing and lake fishing are encouraged. There's even a cleaning station for your fish. From Memorial Day through Labor Day, and the week leading up to Easter, the campground offers a 510-foot long Lazy River, miniature golf course, an outdoor, Olympic-sized pool, a children's pool, paddle boat rentals, a snack bar, an outdoor chapel, an arcade, and a place to rent beach chairs and umbrellas. The chapel has two Sunday services. Lifeguards work on the beach, and the staff plan supervised children's activities daily. ($)

*There are over **450 different hotels** in and around the Myrtle Beach area.*

Outside Myrtle Beach

Myrtle Beach has enough things to see, places to go, and activities to try, that you don't have to consider leaving the city in pursuit of entertainment. Having said that, the rest of the Grand Strand has plenty to offer, so if you have the time, think about expanding your explorations a bit.

The Grand Strand reaches from the North Carolina border and extends 60 miles down to Georgetown, South Carolina. The island is essentially split into three parts: North Strand, Myrtle Beach, and South Strand. Little River, North Myrtle Beach, and Briarcliffe Acres make up North Strand. The South Strand includes Surfside Beach, Garden City Beach, Murrells Inlet, Litchfield Beach, and Pawley's Island.

This chapter lists some attractions, entertainment, and dining options for each community. Because they are all close to each other, it is very easy to make day trips to each of these locations and return to your lodgings in Myrtle Beach afterwards.

NORTH STRAND

Following are a few interesting places to visit on your Grand Strand trip north of Myrtle Beach.

LITTLE RIVER

This fishing village is located right near the border between North and South Carolina. You can schedule deep-sea fishing excursions here, or take a cruise along the Intracoastal Waterway. To get to Little River's waterfront, turn onto Mineola Avenue from US 17.

There are several charter options, such as **Blackfish Charter Boat** (Waterfront Drive; ☎ 843.249.1379), **Little**

River Fishing Fleet (4495 Mineola Avenue; ☏ 843.361.3323; ✆ littleriverfleet.com), and **Longway Charter Fishing** (The Waterfront, 1898 North Twisted Oaks Drive; ☏ 843.249.7813; ✆ longwaycharters.com). Charters run from mid-April to mid-November. The Blackfish and Longway can accommodate parties of up to six. The Little River Fishing Fleet includes Pride of the Carolina, a 90 foot aluminum all-purpose fishing boat, and the Sundancer, a 40 foot fiberglass boat. Half- and full-day trips can be arranged. Some charters offer night fishing, as well. Shark fishing and fishing the Gulf Stream are possible excursions. Bait and tackle are included in charter fees; food and drink are not.

The village also has several public-access marinas that are open year-round. The marinas offer bathhouse facilities and storage. Some even have a restaurant and laundry facilities on the premises.

Some of the local marinas are **Anchor Marina** (2200 Little River Neck Road; ☏ 843.249.7899), **Coquina Harbor** (4208 Coquina Harbor Drive; ☏ 843.249.9333; ✆ coquinayachtclub.com), and **Crickett Cove Marina** (4495 North Baker Street; ☏ 843.249.7169; ✆ crickettcove.com).

Every year in May, the village hosts the **Blue Crab Festival** (☏ 843.249.6604; ✆ crabfestival.com) on the waterfront. The festival showcases live music – jazz, country, bluegrass, and gospel – as well as over 150 arts and crafts booths. For children, there is a petting zoo, pony rides, face-painting, and puppets. There is an admission fee to the festival, even though children under the age of five enter free.

Golfers looking to try courses outside of Myrtle Beach should consider trying out **Glen Dornoch Waterway Golf Links** (US 17 N; ☏ 843.249.2541; ✆ glendornoch.com). Located along the Intracoastal Waterway, the 270-acre course also has pines, oaks, lakes, and a river. The 18-hole, 6035 yard par-72 course was designed by Clyde Johnson to be a tribute to Dornoch, Scotland. At least four holes flank the waterway. The elevation changes are dramatic, such as the 35-foot drops to the water. The course has no wide-open fairways. (Greens fees: $$; no walking)

To get to **Indigo Farms** (☎ 843.399.6902), take S.C. Highway 9 to Loris, and then take S.C. Highway 57 straight to the farm (there are plenty of signs). The farm straddles the North Carolina and South Carolina border. A source of gardening and produce, Indigo Farms has an extensive greenhouse, eat-in bakery and café, and a produce market.

If you are interested in picking your own fruits, Indigo Farms offers strawberries, blueberries, tomatoes, and peaches in season. The farm also holds a Farm Heritage Day on the first or second Saturday in October and a Pumpkin Day on the third Saturday. During Farm Heritage Day, there are presentations on traditional farming methods, farmer games, and history demonstrations (like candle-making!). The games include apple bobbing, hayrides, scarecrow making, and potbelly pig races. For Pumpkin Day, Indigo Farms organizes nighttime hayrides and children draw on pumpkins. Activities vary year to year, so call ahead for a schedule.

Feeling hungry? The **Brentwood Restaurant** (4269 Luck Avenue; ☎ 843.249.2601) offers a gourmet meal that is affordable. The first floor of this remodeled Victorian-style restaurant is devoted to dining. Guests lounge upstairs in a European-style salon and linger over dessert and drinks. The menu includes fresh veal, rack of lamb, fresh local seafood, beef, pork, and duck. All entrees come with fresh bread, salad, a choice of rice pilaf or potatoes, and vegetables. The restaurant also offers a vegetarian menu. Brentwood is open for dinner Monday through Saturday. Reservations are suggested. ($$)

Another option is to go on a casino cruise from Little River. The **Diamond Casino Cruises** (4491 Waterfront Ave; ☎

877.250.LUCK; diamondcasinocruises.com) has two cruises daily, Monday through Sunday. Everyone must be at least 18 years old to board, and 21 to drink. A valid photo ID is required as proof of age before boarding. The cruise offers a variety of games including slots, blackjacks, roulette, dice, and Texas Hold'Em. The cost of the cruise includes free drinks while gambling. There is a buffet on board.

NORTH MYRTLE BEACH

The North Strand's largest municipality is North Myrtle Beach, which was formed by combining four smaller communities: Cherry Grove, Ocean Drive, Crescent Beach, and Windy Hill. The communities all blur together along US 17.

Cherry Grove is just south of Little River and very easy to miss if you aren't paying attention to the signs on US 17 that take you on to the Sea Mountain Highway. Ocean Drive has several clubs along Main Street featuring beach music. Windy Hill Beach has the popular shopping center, Barefoot Landing, and other tourist attractions.

While Atlantic Beach is technically not part of North Myrtle Beach, it is situated between Windy Hill and Crescent Beach. Under the Jim Crow laws that governed most of the South between 1870s and 1960s, Atlantic Beach was the only "black" beach in the area. Blacks were not allowed in any of the other beaches. It's still a predominantly African-American community.

Taking up over 50 acres, **North Myrtle Beach Grand Prix** offers something for everyone in the family. There is a kiddie park with rides for children, a miniature golf course, and a water-race park with bumper boats. Go-karts, mini Ferraris, Jeeps, and Formula 1 racecars, can be tried out on any of the tracks. The park charges ticket fees per ride, but offers free parking. Instead of paying for each ride, you can also get all-you-can-ride armbands or other combo passes. Hours vary be season; the gates are open from 1pm to 11pm in the summer.

The most popular destination in Cherry Grove for shrimping, crabbing with chicken necks, and tending the fish pots is Hogg Inlet. Anglers try out different fishing spots and often try for flounder at night. Hogg Inlet also has some prime shelling grounds. However, unless you are a South Carolina resident, you are out of luck, since the law limits the harvesting to residents without a saltwater fishing license. They can harvest just enough for personal consumption, and in these authorized harvesting areas, the oyster and clam beds cannot be disturbed between May 15 and Sept. 1. The limit is two bushels of oysters, or half a bushel while wading in the water. The local **Department of Health and Environmental Control** (☏ 843.448.1902) provide information on current shellfish bed closings and can answer specific questions.

The fishing pier, **Cherry Grove Pier** (3500 North Ocean Boulevard; ☏ 843.249.1625; ⌨ cherrygrovepier.com), charges daily admission on a per-rod basis. There's also a fee just to walk on the pier. The pier is 985 feet long and has a restaurant and a gift shop carrying a full line of pier tackle. There's also an official weigh station on the pier. Lights allow night fishing off this pier. The pier is open 24 hours a day from March 1 to the Sunday after Thanksgiving.

Golfers should check out **Tidewater Golf Club & Plantation** (4901 Little River Neck Road; ☏ 843.249.3829; ⌨ tidewater.com), a course with scenic vistas overlooking the water. The 560-acre course, located on a seaside peninsula, has views of the Intracoastal Waterway, saltwater marshes, and the Atlantic Ocean. At least one hole is alongside Hogg Inlet so you can watch anglers catching fish. The course is designed in such a way that the only hole you can see is the one you are playing, giving you a sense of privacy as you play. Tidewater has five sets of tees.

Depending on the tee you select, you can stretch this par-72 course from 4765 to 7020 yards. (Green fees: $$$$; walking is permitted)

If you enjoy dancing, shagging is a must. "Shag" refers to a local dance that supposedly originated in Ocean Drive Beach. The best place to dance, or watch others dance, is at **Ducks & Ducks Too** (229 Main Street; ☎ 843.249.3858; ⌐ ducksatoceandrive.com). Shag lessons are often offered, especially during the peak season. Ducks & Ducks Too hosts several shag-inspired events and contests, such as the Dewey Kennedy Mixed Doubles Contest. This club is open Wednesday through Saturday in the summer and from Thursday through Saturday in the winter. The Preliminaries for **the National Shag Dance Championships** (☎ 843.497.7369; ⌐ shagnationals.com) are held in January and the finals are held in March.

There are several popular tourist attractions in Windy Hill Beach, the most well-known one being **Barefoot Landing**. A shopping, dining, and entertainment center built around a 27-acre freshwater lake, Barefoot Landing has more than 100 factory direct stores and retail shops and 13 waterfront restaurants. The complex is situated between US Highway 17 North and the Intracoastal Waterway. There's also a boardwalk along the lake, peppered with rocking chairs, and bridges criss-cross the lake. Nature coexists with commercialism here, with several kinds of water birds and alligators living in the lake.

Speaking of alligators, the 20-acre **Alligator Adventure** (Barefoot Landing; ☎ 843.361.0789; ⌐ alligatoradventure.com) is one of the largest reptilian facilities in the world. Along with 800 alligators, this attraction also is home to exotic birds, frogs, snakes, tortoises, and lizards. A special area of the park, Crocodile Cove, is dedicated to the 13 species of crocodiles. Over 5000 feet of boardwalk weave through the natural wetland habitats that house the animals. The park also hosts shows in the

700-seat amphitheater to teach visitors about the animals in the park.

The park is designed for visitors to wander around themselves, and is also wheelchair accessible. The staff is vigilant about safety. Open year round, ticket prices and hours vary by season. Barefoot Landing is friendly to dogs – as long as they are on a leash, dogs can walk around. There's even a bakery dedicated to dogs, serving freshly baked goodies: **Bone Appetit Bakery** (☎ 843.361.4477).

If you are checking out the shows, make a stop at the **Alabama Theatre** (US 17 N; ☎ 843.272.1111; alabamatheatre.com), also in Barefoot Landing. While there are various productions, the theater is known for its Celebrity Concert series, featuring stars such as Patty Loveless, Kenny Chesney, and of course, Alabama (the theater's namesake).

SOUTH STRAND

The pace of life here is decidedly more leisurely. Compared to Myrtle Beach and North Myrtle Beach, South Strand has decidedly less neon and less glitter. The prime attraction is Mother Nature – with rich marshland, inlets, and the maritime forest.

SURFSIDE BEACH
Immediately adjacent to Myrtle Beach, the town of Surfside Beach is the most like the city in the glittery attractions. For nostalgia-seekers, the **Legends in Concert** (301 US 17 Business S; ☎ 843.238.7827; legendsinconcertsc.com) is something to try. A live on-stage recreation of performances by some of the biggest names in music, such as Dolly Parton, the Blues Brothers, Elton John, Madonna, and Elvis Presley, the show is a fun look at the past. The impersonators don't just have uncanny resemblances in their act, they are also able to mimic the voices and move-

ments. The show is live in every sense – there is no lip-syncing. The theater has state of the art sound, lighting, and multimedia special effects to deliver a spectacular production. The annual Christmas show is also popular.

The **Wild Water & Race Theme Park** (910 US 17 S; ☏ 843.238.3787) combines water parks with go-karts. The 16-acre park has a number of water rides and slides, such as the Dark Hole, a fully enclosed tube ride, the Sidewinder and Serpentine body flumes, the 65-foot high Free Fall Cliff Dive, and the 65-foot-high Triple Dip Speed Slide. A 16-foot-wide Lazy River meanders through a rain forest and waterfalls as it traverses the entire length of the park. There's also a kid's park with a pool and slides.

The other side of the park features five racetracks. Everyone from toddlers to adults can get on the tracks. Finally, the park offers bumper boats and an 18-hole miniature golf course. Open for the season in early May, the park closes by mid-September. The park is open daily from 10 AM to 7 PM

Golfers should check out **Wicked Stick** (US 17 Bypass; ☏ 843.215.2500; 🖱 wickedstick.com), a course designed by John Daly and Clyde Johnston. The links style course has wide-open spaces featuring large sand waste areas, deep pot bunkers, and water hazards. The par-72 course measures 6080 yards – over 7000 yards from the championship tees. (Green fees $$$; walking permitted in late afternoon if not too busy)

Fishermen (and women) can trot down to **Surfside Pier** (11 South Ocean Boulevard) to try their luck. This 810 foot long pier charges admission for each angler and spectator. If you are staying for a while, weekly or seasonal passes may be worthwhile. Tackle and bait are available on the pier, along with rod-and-reel rentals. The tackle shop and the pier are open 24 hours a day from March to mid-December. There's also an official weigh station here.

GARDEN CITY BEACH

A family-oriented beach, surf fishing is very popular in this part of the South Strand. While the **Pier at Garden City** (110 South Waccamaw Drive; ☎ 843.651.9700; pieratgardencity.com) is generally open everyday, 24 hours a day, from March to December, daily hours may sometimes vary. The café on the pier is closed from Christmas to April, however. The pier charges daily admission for each angler but allows spectators to walk out on to the pier for free. Season passes are available. The tackle shop provides bait and rental gear. There is an official weight station here.

MURRELLS INLET

The oldest fishing village in South Carolina, Murrells Inlet is claimed by locals as the "seafood capital of the Carolinas." Murrells Inlet has prime shelling grounds accessible without a boat. However, unless you are a South Carolina resident, you are out of luck, since the law limits the harvesting to residents without a saltwater fishing license. They can harvest just enough for personal consumption, and in these authorized harvesting areas, the oyster and clam beds cannot be disturbed between May 15 and Sept. 1.

The limit is two bushels of oysters, or half a bushel while wading in the water. The local **Department of Health and Environmental Control** (☎ 843.448.1902) provides information on current shellfish bed closings and can answer specific questions. Fishing is possible in the creeks and waterways, however.

Captain Dick's Marina (4123 US 17 S; ☎ 843.651.3676; captdicks.com) offers charters for deep-sea bottom fishing. All the boats feature air-conditioned cabins and full food service. Trips can range anywhere from five hours to a whole day, and is priced accordingly. Rods, manual reels, bait, and tackle are provided on short trips. Electric reels are available only on longer trips. The marina takes care of the fishing licenses. The marina also offers the Captain Dick's Saltwater Marsh Explorer Cruises. The discovery tour explores the marshes and discusses the plants, animals (like the dolphins!), birds, and marine life that live here. There's also a fishing demonstration and a walk along a barrier island.

One of the best reasons to venture down to Murrells Inlet, **Brookgreen Gardens** (US Hwy 17; ☎ 843.235.6000; brookgreen.org) is located 20 miles south of Myrtle Beach. Created in 1931 by Archer and Anna Hyatt Huntington, this nonprofit outdoor garden has over 550 sculpture pieces and 2000 species and subspecies of plants. Originally, the property was part of four rice plantations and saw many famous faces in its history. Francis Marion, the South's legendary guerrilla leader during the Revolutionary War, spent time on these waterways, and George Washington spent a night here in 1791. Washington Allston, a famous painter, was born here in 1779. Theodosia Alston, daughter of Aaron Burr lived on one of the plantations. Carolina golden big-grain rice was discovered and cultivated here.

This self-supporting outdoor museum includes wide lawns and intimate gardens. The gardens include oaks, magnolias, wildflowers, and some exotic species, like the propagated azaleas and camellias. There are bronze and marble sculptures, as well as fountains.

The 50-acre wildlife refuge on the premises has a variety of animals, including alligators, otters, eagles, wild turkeys, and deer, in their native habitats. Some of the habitats are the Cypress Aviary, Otter Pond, Alligator Swamp, Fox Glade, Raptor Aviary, and the White-tailed Deer Savannah.

Food and drinks are available at the Terrace Café and picnic areas are available. There is also an education center with an exhibition hall and auditorium, where classes and demonstrations are often held.

Children under the age of five go in for free. There are discounts for senior citizens, young adults (13 to 18) and children (6 to 12). The gardens are wheelchair accessible, and wheelchairs are also provided upon request. The admission ticket is valid up to seven consecutive days since the date of purchase.

Memberships are also available. Walking tours are included in the admission price, although visitors can opt to walk through on their own. Tour guides are available for an additional fee.

The Trekker is an overland vehicle offering an hour of driving the back roads and trails. The 48-foot-pontoon boat, The Springfield, explores the waterways, cypress swamps, and abandoned rice fields.

Brookgreen is open daily year-round during normal business hours, and sometimes open on evenings for special events. The gardens are closed on Mondays in December and on Christmas Day. No pets are allowed at the gardens.

Golfers can look to play at **Blackmoor Golf Club** at Longwood Plantation (SC 707; ☎ 866.952.5555; ✆ blackmoor.com). The course flanks the Waccamaw River and is designed to take advantage of the terrain. No 14 has water on one side and sand traps on the other side of the fairway. The green is 285 yards from the tee. The 8th hole is a split fairway and trees flank both sides. Blackmoor is a 6,533 yards and par-72 course. (Green fees: $$$; no walking)

Antiquing is popular here, and antique stores line US 17 Business and Bypass. There's the **Wachesaw Row Antique Mall**, south of Inlet Square Mall on US 17 Business, where you can pick up a brochure that lists all area antique shops. A&G Furniture is a 9,000 square foot outlet of antiques, furniture, glassware, clocks, books, and collectibles. Legacy Antique Mall carries estate jewelry, silver, and paintings.

LITCHFIELD BEACH

US 17 at this point passes through dense woodland and manicured landscapes. The area was originally named Magnolia Beach; Litchfield refers to a **rice plantation** (Litchfield Plantation; King's River Road; ☎ 843.237.9121; ⌀ litchfieldplantation.com) on the Waccamaw River. The manor house is still standing, and currently operates as a country club and a bed-and-breakfast inn. The town has many small shops and restaurants. The beaches here are among the widest, cleanest, and best preserved on the Carolina coast. However, most of the beach is private; there are only a few public access points here.

PAWLEY'S ISLAND

South of Litchfield, Pawley's Island was a summer retreat for wealthy plantation owners and their families even as far back as the 1700s. Like Litchfield, the beaches here are among the widest, cleanest, and best-preserved on the Carolina coast. Again, most of the beach is private; there are only a few public access points here.

The **Hobcaw Barony Nature Center** (US 17; ☎ 843.546.4623) features displays and audiovisual programs on local history, wildlife, and coastal environment. The center has a saltwater touch tank and snake displays. As there are no walking trails or self-guided tours, reservations are required for guided tours and special programs. Open year round, admission is free to this center.

GEORGETOWN

A shipping community formerly known as Little Charleston, Georgetown marks the end of the Grand Strand. The area retains a Revolutionary War era flavor with its narrow brick streets and old churches dating back two centuries. The town's bell-towered **Rice Museum** (633 Front Street; ☎ 843.546.7423; ⌀

ricemuseum.com) covers the antebellum history of the plantations. The museum is open year round Monday to Saturday from 10AM to 4:30PM. It is closed on major holidays.

A reservation is required to visit **Mansfield Plantation** (1776 Mansfield Road; ☎ 843.546.6961; ✆ mansfieldplantation.com). Even then, tours require a group of twelve or more.

Approximately 100 slaves worked the antebellum plantation. Visitors can now see the slave village, the chapel, the old rice fields, and the winnowing building (where rice was separate from chaff), in addition to the mansion. There are three different kinds of tours.

Twelve miles to the south is **Hopsewee Plantation** (494 Hopsewee Road; ☎ 843.546.7891; ✆ hopsewee.com), a mansion typical of the 18th Century rice plantation manors. The residence features four rooms opening into a wide central hall on each floor. The attic rooms and the brick cellar are also open for viewing.

Recommendations

This section is intended to help Myrtle Beach visitors gather ideas for different vacation possibilities; to plan the vacation that best suits them. Whether visitors are seeking the perfect golf outing, a restful beach vacation, or a family reunion, this section can help guide them in the right direction.

Travel Scenarios

Interested in a golf vacation? There are hotels and travel agents ready to help you plan the perfect golf vacation. But perhaps you are not a golfer, or you are looking to do something other than golfing. If that is the case, this chapter, with suggested itineraries to fit your particular vacation preferences, is for you.

SHORT STAY
Perhaps you are in Myrtle Beach only for two days, such as a weekend, and don't really have a lot of time. In that case, get a hotel right on the beach, along Ocean Boulevard. The accommodations chapter will help you find the best lodging to fit your budget. The sun sparkling on the water as the waves roll in is a nice view to enjoy from the room while getting ready for the day. Spend the morning on the beach before it gets too hot and crowded. If you enjoy fishing, head down to one of the fishing piers in the morning to stake out a nice spot. Afterwards, head for the **Broadway at the Beach** complex and spend the hottest hours of the day in the cool air of **Ripley's Aquarium**. There are plenty of lunch options at the complex, as well as other activities, such as **Dragon Lair** miniature golf course. As the afternoon winds down, make sure you have your show tickets for the night. Broadway at the Beach has several tourist offices where

helpful staffers would be delighted to help you decide which show you are interested in and to assist you in procuring the tickets. If it isn't a dinner show, you may want to consider checking out some of the restaurants up by Restaurant Row. If you are still looking for more after the show, check out the Dueling Pianos at the **Crocodile Rocks Dueling Pianos Saloon** at Broadway at the Beach's Celebrity Circle. Dance the night away at several of the clubs or relax in your room as you watch the ocean.

For your second, and final, day, consider checking out some of the area amusement parks. Although the Pavilion is gone, Myrtle Beach still has plenty of rides and water parks that will make the entire day disappear. If amusement parks aren't your cup of tea, there are other similar attractions clustered around the parks on Ocean Boulevard. An example is **the Ripley's *Believe It or Not!* Museum**. Don't forget to take advantage of the pool or Lazy River or other water entertainment back at your hotel (if your hotel has water activities available).

OFF-SEASON

Perhaps you are in Myrtle Beach during the off-season – all the amusement parks are closed, and you don't really like amusement parks anyway. Traditionally, most Myrtle Beach businesses were closed during the winter, but that is beginning to change. As more and more people make Myrtle Beach their home year round, and as more and more visitors look at Myrtle Beach as a possible tourist destination in the winter, more places are beginning to stay open. **Broadway at the Beach** is ready to welcome all winter visitors – zip around the racetrack a few times at **NASCAR Speed Park**, eat and drink aboard the boat-shaped **Margaritaville** restaurant, and tear into steak at **TBonz Steakhouse**. **Ripley's Aquarium** has shows everyday and the sharks are always happy for visitors. **The Crab House** is an excellent dinner choice – and a visit to the tourist office beforehand can score you a few coupons that you can use on your meal. While the water would be a little too chilly for a swim, the weather is generally nice enough to enjoy spending time on the sand.

There are umbrellas and chairs on parts of the beach and many of the oceanfront hotels offer deck chairs that you can drag onto the sand. In the morning and afternoon, you will find plenty of sunbathers relaxing on towels on the beach.

Generally show tickets are easier to get during the off-season, but if you are trying to get tickets to the Christmas shows, all bets are off. The Christmas season is fairly busy for the entertainment industry at Myrtle Beach, so many of the shows are sold out. However, outside the Christmas season, many of the popular shows offer more available seats. The **Palace Theater** and **Carolina Opry** are some of the places you can consider.

If dancing is not your style, would a sports bar be more your thing? There are sports bars scattered through the city where you can enjoy a couple drinks and your favorite sporting event on one of the multiple TV screens.

ROMANTIC GETAWAY
Perhaps you are in Myrtle Beach as a romantic getaway for you and a special someone. Consider some of the high-end lodging options listed in the accommodations chapter. It would be recommended to check out some of the resorts. Many of the resorts offer units with kitchens and private areas, giving you the option to have a cozy evening "at home" during your vacation. The resorts also often plan various activities that may be of interest, as well as offering access to several pools, hot tubs, and Lazy River rides. Enjoy lazing around poolside.

The beach gets pretty crowded during the day, so in the early mornings and in the late afternoons, as the day begins to cool off, take the time to walk down to the beach, sit on the sand, or just relax and watch the waves roll in.

The local paper would be able to tell you if there are any musical performances happening during your stay, such as the concert series offered by The **Trinity Episcopal Church** and the **First Presbyterian Church**. There are other musical groups, such as the Coastal Concert Association and the Carolina Master Chorale.

If you are part of the couple that enjoys dressing up and going out for dinner, an evening of fine dining at **The Library** or **Sea Island** may be fun. Both places require dressy attire, but promise (and deliver) excellent food and drink in a classy and elegant atmosphere. For more casual couples, a good steakhouse, such as **New York Prime**, would be more appropriate.

While shows at the **Carolina Opry** (or similar locations) may be spectacular and thrilling, it's not for everyone. How about an evening of comedy at the **Comedy Cabana**? The club has new acts and require only a two-drinks minimum.

The romantic couple should also consider venturing out of Myrtle Beach a little and exploring the nearby communities. Shag dancing originated in North Myrtle Beach and there are clubs devoted to this local dance. **Ducks** & **Ducks Too** often offers lessons – even if there aren't any actual lessons, there are always plenty of people willing to teach you.

Along with other shows and theaters in the area, a visit to historic **Georgetown** is suggested. There's nothing more romantic than visiting former antebellum plantations and feeling the town's Revolutionary War era flavor.

FAMILY VACATION

Perhaps you are visiting Myrtle Beach with kids in tow. Never fear! Myrtle Beach has plenty of engage and interest children of all ages. For families, a resort setting might also be helpful. The accommodations would often include a cooking area for snacks and a private area to unwind after a day of activities. Many resorts also plan activities geared toward children. The resort is also a more controlled environment for children wanting to splash around in the water. If a resort is not possible, perhaps camping out might be an option.

Ripley's Aquarium at **Broadway at the Beach** would intrigue even the most jaded child. Petting the sting rays and watching the horseshoe crabs evoke giggles. Walking through the Dangerous Reef tank and being surrounded by multi-colored schools of fish would amaze, and there may be several gasps of surprise when they look up and see a shark swimming right over them. The aquarium also offers children's activities, such as the sleepover.

The **Children's Museum** offers a variety of exhibits, such as the Discovery Lab, Circuit Center, and Fairway Physics, to combine science with fun. The hospital exhibit teaches kids what happens inside a hospital. With over 7,000 square feet of interactive displays, parents and children will both enjoy exploring and learning about science.

Even if you don't end up checking out any of the local amusement parks such as **Family Kingdom**, **NASCAR Speed Park**, or **Myrtle Waves**, it's worth heading to North Myrtle Beach for the **Grand Prix**. The Kiddie Park has rides for children, a miniature golf course, and a water-race park with bumper boats. And since you are already venturing out of the city, what's to stop the kids from hanging out with alligators at **Alligator Adventure** in Barefoot Landing? One of the world's largest reptilian facility, children will enjoy meandering through the park looking at alligators, crocodiles, lizards, and frogs. There are shows held daily in the amphitheater.

There are other animals to see at Myrtle Beach. First, the Butterfly Pavilion. The best part of the pavilion would probably be crawling through the beehive to see the honeybees make honey. Children will also enjoy seeing the collection of exotic and domestic animals at the **Waccatee Zoological Farm**. There are Bengal tigers, lions, bears, monkeys, zebras, and deer. If the kids are old enough to sit still for a prolonged period of time, perhaps **Medieval Times** or **Dixie Stampede** would be a nice combination of dinner and show.

Give your child them a chance to feel the power of their favorite fantasy stories by giving them their very own wand at **MagiQuest**, at Broadway at the Beach. Let them use their wands to cast spells and defeat magical creatures, complete quests, and discover treasure. MagiQuest harnesses imagination in an interactive game for children.

EDUCATIONAL EXPERIENCE
Perhaps you enjoy history and the arts? Or perhaps you are more interested in nature. Myrtle Beach is blessed with both. The **South Carolina Hall of Fame** focuses on the state's history. Local parks often have visual art exhibits throughout the year. And the **Franklin G. Burroughs and Simeon B. Chapin Art Museum** showcases local and national artists in ten galleries. A visit to historic Georgetown will feel like traveling back to the Revolutionary War era, walking down narrow brick streets and ducking into churches built during the colonial days. The **Rice Museum** covers the antebellum history of the plantations. There are also several former rice plantations nearby that offer tours of the buildings and the fields.

While communing with Mother Nature on the beach or on the fishing pier would score you a suntan, and some fish, perhaps you want a different experience. Nature-oriented attractions, such as the **Butterfly Pavilion**, **Ripley's Aquarium**, and **Alligator Adventure** (at Barefoot Landing) would introduce you to a wide variety of animal habitats. You would discover plants and statues at **Brookgreen Gardens** (at Murrels Inlet).

If you are looking for nature tours, there are safari jeep tours that would give you an overview of the area history and show off natural coastal attractions. A jaunt up to Little River would give you the opportunity to go on a boat and explore the Intracoastal Waterways. Brookgreen Gardens also offers tours aboard The Trekker, an overland vehicle, and aboard The Springfield, a 48-foot pontoon boat, to explore the waterways, cypress swamps, and abandoned rice fields.

Nature fans shouldn't miss the 312-acre **Myrtle Beach State Park**. There's a nature trail and a nature center where a park naturalist conducts activities year-round.

AUTHOR RECOMMENDATIONS

This book is intended to be a guide during your visit. There are many things to see and do here that no book can list them all. Instead, as a guide, the book can point you in the right direction as you explore and enjoy yourself. This chapter highlights specific places that should find room on your Myrtle Beach itinerary.

RIPLEY'S AQUARIUM
The big must-see at Broadway at the Beach is Ripley's Aquarium. From the outside, it is just steel and concrete. Inside, however, is a $40 million state-of-the-art educational marine facility offering educational exhibits that is both entertaining and fun.

For most people, the name "Ripley" conjures images of weird and surprising artifacts and exhibits. That isn't the case with the aquarium. It has a different feel, layout, and content from the other Ripley's attractions in that it isn't trying to creep you out or make you doubt what you are seeing. Instead, the aquarium is involved with environment education, conservation, and research. Ticket prices add up for large groups, so look into discounts – such as online coupons, military ID, and student ID.

The aquarium is pretty small – you can see and enjoy most of the exhibits in a little over an hour if it isn't too crowded. Even with crowds, the aquarium has done a good job of arranging the exhibits so that the traffic generally flows in one direction. The ocean-life, while not as extensive as aquariums in bigger cities, such as nearby Atlanta or Baltimore, is still varied. Rio Amazon displays piranha and other fish found in the Amazon River. The exhibits include the giant octopus, sea anemones, coral, jellyfish, seahorse, horseshoe crabs, and rays. At the Sea-For-Yourself Discovery Center, you can hold a horseshoe crab or pet a gentle ray. There are dive shows and marine education classes.

If you are on a tight timeframe, just make the time to experience "Dangerous Reef" a 750,000-gallon tank with a 330 feet tunnel going through the tanks. A moving glide path takes you through the tunnel, giving you a view of the fish, rays, eels, and sharks. Look up – you may see the shark swim right over your head. The tunnel provides a unique perspective of the ocean floor.

THE PALACE THEATRE
Secondly, the Palace Theatre is a beautiful structure on its own, with lights illuminating the building's façade at night. The lobby is very nicely decorated and has three chandeliers. On the outside, lights transform the building. The Palace Theatre is a twenty million dollar, 2,638 seat facility built in 1995 in the center of Myrtle Beach. It is part of the award-winning entertainment complex "Broadway At The Beach". There are shows every night.

CAROLINA OPRY

For shows, the Carolina Opry is also a must. As the area's first successful theater, the Carolina Opry helped build the city's show industry. The two-hour variety show is a true mixture, with a little bit of country music, a dash of jazz, a pinch of Nashville, a smattering of Broadway, and some sparkles of Vegas. The "Good Vibrations" show is fun and feels like a ride on the time machine as the cast sings and dances to music from the 60s, 70s, and 80s.

LEGENDS IN CONCERT

Another show worth making the time to see is the "Legends in Concert" show at Surfside Beach. Even though Legends in Concert is outside of Myrtle Beach, it is worth venturing out to catch the glittery show. Impersonators of major musical performers, such as Dolly Parton, Madonna, and Elvis Presley, deliver a fun and delightful show straight out of the past. The theater delivers a technically spectacular production, as well, with state-of-the-art sound, lighting, and special effects.

BROOKGREEN GARDENS

Another should-not-miss attraction outside of the city is the Brookgreen Gardens. In nearby Murrels Inlet, the non-profit outdoor gardens were part of a rice plantation. The gardens feature a wide variety of flowering plants and trees, and not all of them are native to the area. The 50-acre wildlife refuge has several animal habitats. Bronze and marble sculptures and fountains dot the gardens.

MAGIQUEST

Back in Myrtle Beach, if you have time to kill and enjoy Harry Potter, Lord of the Rings, or other fantasy worlds, MagiQuest is a great way to pass the time. A form of role-playing, MagiQuest is an indoor interactive game where you go on quests and adventures. The duels in the gift shop are a great chance to try out different spells on your friends. The IMAX Theater and the Dragon's Lair Minature Golf are also worth checking out if you have the time to spare.

MYRTLE BEACH PELICANS
The true sports fan – especially baseball fans – should make the effort to see the Myrtle Beach Pelicans play during the summer. Class-A games are very different from the major leagues – there are less base hits, less dramatic home runs, and less arguing with the referees. Old-timers would remember the Myrlte Beach Hurricanes, the class-A affiliate of the Toronto Blue Jays, that left town in 1992. The Atlanta Braves brought the Pelicans to town in 1999. As part of the Carolina League, the Pelicans play rivals such as the Wilmington Blue Rocks (class-A team for the Kansas City Royals), Lynchburg Hillcats, and the Kinston Indians. A very popular place for families, even young children can enjoy watching the games and Dinger the Home Run Dog between innings. Many of the "Birds" moved up to the Braves during the course of the season. Former Braves second-baseman and National League all-star Marcus Giles started with the Pelicans, as did former Braves shortstop Rafael Furcal, former pitcher Horacio Ramirez, former first-baseman Adam LaRoche, and former pitcher Jose Capellan. Current starting pitcher Chuck James began with the Pelicans in the 2005 season and made his major league debut against the Colorado Rockies that September. The Pelicans have a very successful list of players that have made it to the majors, so you will get the chance to see the future stars before they appear in the Braves uniform.

*The magazine **Sports Illustrated** got its start at the Pine Lakes Country Club in Myrtle Beach.*

Index

2

2001 VIP Entertainment, 115

A

accommodations, 153
accommodations (Broadway at the Beach), 172
Adventure Water Sports, 59
Akel's House of Pancakes, 128
annual events, 45
Anything Joe's, 149
Apache Family Campgrounds, 175
Apache Pier, 67
Arcadian Shores Golf Club, 76
Arrowhead Country Club, 76

B

bars, sports, 117
Beach Ball Classic, 51
Beach Colony Resort, 158
Beach Wagon, 116
beaches, 53
Belle Terre Golf Course, 77
Best View Farm, 102
bike rentals, 101
Bi-Lo Myrtle Beach Marathon, 47
Blackmoor Golf Club, 193
boat, getting there by, 35
boating, 60
boating rules, 61
Breakers Resort, 159
Broadway at the Beach, 139
Broadway Louie's Grill, 148
Brookgreen Gardens, 192
Budweiser Boat Show, The Grand Strand, 46
Bullwinkle's Family Food and Fun, 146
Bummz on the Beach, 117
Burroughs & Chapin Golf Management, 73
Burroughs, F. A., 24
bus, getting there by, 34
Butterfly Pavilion, 143

C

Caddyshack (Restaurant), 145
Cagney's Old Place, 128
Canadian-American Days, 48
Cane Patch, 84
Captain Dick's Marina, 191
Captain Hook's Adventure Golf, 85
car, getting around by, 36
car, getting there by, 33
Carolina Opry, 108
Carolina Roadhouse, 129
Carolina Safari Jeep Tours, 96
Carousel Park (Broadway at the Beach), 142
Chapin Park, 101
Chestnut Hill, 128
Children's Museum of South Carolina, 91
Christmas Elegance, 136
City Bait & Tackle, 68
clams, 66
Classics of Myrtle Beach, 72
Club Boca, 150
Coastal Grand Mall, 135

Collector's Cafe and Gallery, 126
Colonial Mall Myrtle Beach, 135
Comedy Cabana, 110
Coral Beach Resort, 160
crabbing, 66
Crocodile Rocks Dueling Pianos, 151

D

Dagwoods, 129
Days Inn Myrtle Beach, 174
Dead Dog Saloon, 116
Dickens Christmas Show/Festival, 51
Dirty Don's Oyster Bar & Grill, 122
Dixie Stampede, Dolly Parton, 108
Doll Show, 49
Downwind Sails, 58, 60
Dragon's Lair Fantasy Golf, 143
Driftwood Lodge, 155
Droopy's, 117
Dunes Golf and Beach Club, 77

F

Factory Stores, Myrtle Beach, 134
Family Kingdom, 92
Fiesta Del Burro Loco, 125
fishing, 63
Fishing Rodeo, Grand Strand, 49
Fitness One-on-One, 103
Flamingo Seafood Grill, 123
Foster's Cafe & Bar, 118
Franklin G. Burroughs and Simeon B. Chapin Art Museum, 91
Froggy Bottomz, 151

G

Garden City Beach, 191
Gay Dolphin, 136
Georgetown, 194
golf, 71
Golf Holiday)Myrtle Beach), 72
Golf Trips, 45
Grand Dunes Tennis Club, 103
Grand Strand Senior for the Performing Arts, 113
Grand Strand Yoga, 102
Grand Strand, about the, 29
Grande Dunes Golf Course, 78

H

Hague Marina, 59
Hampton Inn Myrtle Beach, 173
Hard Rock Cafe, 144
Hard Rock Park, 96
Hilton Myrtle Beach, 161
history, Myrtle Beach, 23
Hobcaw Barony Nature Center, 194
Holiday Inn at the Pavilion, 157
Holiday Inn Express, 173
Hopsewee Plantation, 195
House of Blues, 112
hurricanes, 41

I

Independence Day, 50
information, getting, 31

J

Jimmagan's Pub, 118
Jimmy Buffett's Margaritaville, 144
Joe's Crab Shack, 148

Jungle Lagoon, 85
Jungle Safari Mini Golf, 85
Jurassic Adventure Golf, 85

K

Kingston Plantation, 162
Koto Japanese Steak House, 148

L

La Plage, 137
La Quinta In and Suites, 175
Lakewood Camping Resort, 176
Legends Complex, 78
Liberty Steakhouse and Brewery, 146
Library (restaurant), 125
lifeguards, 54
Lifestyle Expo, 45
Litchfield Beach, 194
Little River, 183
Long Bay Symphony, 113

M

MagiQuest, 141
Malibou's Surf Bar, 151
Man O'War, 79
Mansfield Plantation, 195
Mardi Gras, 47
Margaritaville (Restaurant), 144
Marvin's, 118
Medieval Times Dinner and Tournament, 111
Midway Par 3 Golf, 84
miniature golf, 85
Mother Fletcher's, 116
Murphy's Law (Bar), 118
Murrells Inlet, 191
Music City Grille, 147

Myrtle Beach Area Convention and Visitors Bureau, 31
Myrtle Beach National, 79
Myrtle Beach Public Courts, 103
Myrtle Beach Speedway, 104
Myrtle Beach State Park, 99, 177
Myrtle Beach State Park, fishing in, 67
Myrtle Beach Travel Park, 178
Myrtle Beach Water Sports, 58
Myrtle Square Area, 135
Myrtle Waves, 95
Myrtlewood Golf Club, 80

N

NASCAR Cafe (Restaurant), 145
NASCAR Speedpark, 93
NASCAR Speedpark Challenge Golf, 86
National Retired Miliary Golf Classic, 74
National Shag Dance Championships, 46
New York Prime, 123
newspapers, 39
nightlife, 114
North Myrtle Beach, 186

O

Ocean Dunes Resort, 168
Ocean Forest Plaza, 169
Ocean Forest Villas, 170
Ocean Lakes Family Campground, 178
Ocean Watersports, 59
offshore fishing, 64
orientation, 29
Osprey Marina, 59
oysters, 66

P

Palace Resort, 163
Palace Theatre, 142
parks, city, 100
Pavilion Amusement Park, 89
Pawley's Island, 194
Pelicans (sports team), 104
Pepper Geddings Recreation
    Center, 102
pets, bringing, 38
PGA Tour Superstore, 73
Pine Lakes International, 80
Pirateland Family Campground,
    179
Pirates Watch, 86
plane, getting there by, 33
Planet Hollywood, 146
Prestwick Country Club, 81
Prime Times Golf & Travel, 73
public transporation, getting
    around by, 36

R

Rainbow Falls, 86
Rainbow Harbor, 136
Revolutions Retro Dance Club,
    150
Rice Museum, 194
Ripley's Aquarium, 140
Ripley's Believe It or Not!
    Museum, 90
River City Cafe, 130
River Oaks Golf Plantation, 81
River Street Sweets, 149
Rossi's, 127
rules, beach, 55
Run to the Sun, 48

S

safety, beach, 53
Sail & Ski Connection, 57
Sam Snead's Tavern, 127
Sand Dunes Resort, 171
Sands Beach Club, 170
Sands Ocean Club, 172
Sands Resorts, 167
Sea Captain's House, 123
Sea Crest Oceanfront Resort, 164
Sea Island, 126
Sea Island Inn, 156
Sea Mist Oceanfront Resort, 165
seasons, 40
Second Avenue Pier and
    Restaurant, 68
Serendipity Inn, 157
Shamrock's (Bar & Grill), 119
Sheraton Broadway Plantation,
    173
Sheraton Myrtle Beach
    Convention Center Hotel, 166
Shipwreck Island Adventure Golf,
    86
shopping, 133
shows, live, 107
South Carolina Hall of Fame, 91
Springmaid Pier, 68
Spyglass, 86
Studebaker's, 117
Summer Family Golf Tournament,
    76
Sun Fun Festival, 50
Surf City, 57
surf fishing, 63
surfing, 56
Surfside Beach, 189

T

Tanger Outlets, 134
taxi, getting around by, 36
T-Bonz Gill & Grill, 124
temperatures, 40
Thorny's Steakhouse & Saloon, 124
Tony Roma's, 147
train, getting there by, 34
travel agents, 32
Treasure Island, 87

V

Veterans Golf Classic, 75
Veteran's Golf Classic, 49
Villa Mare, 125
Vintage House Cafe, 129

W

Waccamaw Factory Shoppes, 134
Waccatee Zoological Farm, 97
Wachesaw Row Antique Mall, 193
water sports, 56
waterskiing, 57
Waterway Hills, 82
Whispering Pines, 82
Wild Wing Plantation, 83
Wizard Golf, 83
World Amateur Golf Championship, 50

X

X-Treme Surf & Skateboard, 58

About the Author

Fahmida Y. Rashid is a technology journalist living in New York City. When not writing about security management and data storage, she is busy planning her next trip, or reading about other adventurers. She has traveled extensively throughout Asia, North Africa, and Europe, and the U.S. She enjoys immersing herself in the area, participating in festivals and celebrations, and dining on local cuisine.

TOURIST TOWN GUIDES™

Explore America's Fun Places

Books in the *Tourist Town Guides*™ series are available at bookstores and online. You can also visit our website for additional, updated book and travel information. The address is:

http://www.touristtown.com

Atlantic City (3rd Edition)

Millions of people visit this vacation destination each year. But there is so much more to Atlantic City than just casinos.

Price: $14.95; ISBN: 978-0-9792043-0-2

Gatlinburg

Not just the "gateway to the Smokies" anymore, Gatlinburg is a favorite vacation destination in one of America's most beautiful regions.

Price: $14.95; ISBN: 978-0-9792043-2-6

Jackson Hole

The spirit of the American West is alive and well in Jackson Hole, and this independent guidebook will help give you the insight on the area's very best.

Price: $14.95; ISBN: 978-0-9792043-3-3

Key West

There is much to see and do Key West. From beaches to restaurants to nightlife, this book will help plan your Conch Republic vacation.

Price: $14.95; ISBN: 978-0-9792043-4-0

Las Vegas (2nd Edition)

The city has become synonymous with the American ideals of vacation and pleasure. But there is much more to Las Vegas than casinos!

Price: $14.95; ISBN: 978-0-9792043-5-7

Myrtle Beach

It is a city that has become the American answer to a tropical paradise. With this completely independent guide, get the insight on the best of Myrtle Beach.

Price: $14.95; ISBN: 978-0-9792043-6-4

Niagara Falls (2nd Edition)

There is so much more to Niagara than just the falls. Whether on your first or tenth visit, this guide will help you explore the many wonders that the area has to offer.

Price: $14.95; ISBN: 978-0-9792043-7-1

Wisconsin Dells (2nd Edition)

With waterparks, wax museums, and so much to offer visitors, Wisconsin Dells is indeed a classic American vacation destination.

Price: $13.95; ISBN: 978-0-9792043-9-5

TOURIST TOWN GUIDES™
www.touristtown.com

**ORDER FORM #1
ON REVERSE SIDE**

Tourist Town Guides™ is published by:

CHANNEL LAKE
Book and Media Publishers

Channel Lake, Inc.
P.O. Box 1771
New York, NY 10156

TOURIST TOWN GUIDES™
ORDER FORM

Telephone: With your credit card handy, call toll-free 800.592.1566

Fax: Send this form toll-free to 866.794.5507

E-mail: Send the information on this form to orders@channellake.com

Postal mail: Send this form with payment to Channel Lake, Inc. P.O. Box 1771, New York, NY, 10156

Your Information: ( ) Do not add me to your mailing list

Name: _____

Address: _____

City: _____ State: _____ Zip: _____

Telephone: _____

E-mail: _____

Book Title(s) / ISBN(s) / Quantity / Price
(see previous pages or www.touristtown.com for this information)

_____

_____

_____

Total payment*: $_____

Payment Information: (Circle One)   Visa / Mastercard

Number: _____ Exp: _____

Or, make check payable to: **Channel Lake, Inc.**

*Add $3.00 per order for domestic shipping, regardless of the quantity ordered. International orders call or e-mail first! New York orders add 8% sales tax.

TOURIST TOWN GUIDES™
www.touristtown.com

ORDER FORM #2
ON REVERSE SIDE

(for additional orders)

Tourist Town Guides™ is published by:

CHANNEL LAKE
Book and Media Publishers

Channel Lake, Inc.
P.O. Box 1771
New York, NY 10156

TOURIST TOWN GUIDES™
ORDER FORM

Telephone: With your credit card handy, call toll-free 800.592.1566

Fax: Send this form toll-free to 866.794.5507

E-mail: Send the information on this form to orders@channellake.com

Postal mail: Send this form with payment to Channel Lake, Inc. P.O. Box 1771, New York, NY, 10156

Your Information: ( ) Do not add me to your mailing list

Name: _____

Address: _____

City: _____ State: _____ Zip: _____

Telephone: _____

E-mail: _____

Book Title(s) / ISBN(s) / Quantity / Price
(see previous pages or www.touristtown.com for this information)

_____

_____

_____

Total payment*: $_____

Payment Information: (Circle One) Visa / Mastercard

Number: _____ Exp: _____

Or, make check payable to: **Channel Lake, Inc.**

*Add $3.00 per order for domestic shipping, regardless of the quantity ordered. International orders call or e-mail first! New York orders add 8% sales tax.